A Manager's Guide to Local Networks

Frank J. Derfler, Jr.
William Stallings

A SPECTRUM BOOK

PRENTICE-HALL, INC.
Englewood Cliffs, New Jersey 07632

Library of Congress Cataloging in Publication Data

Derfler, Frank J.
    A manager's guide to local networks.

    "A Spectrum Book."
    Includes index.
    1. Computer networks.   2. Office practice—Automation.
I. Stallings, William.   II. Title.
TK5105.5.D47   1983   001.64′404   82-21566
ISBN 0-13-549766-3
ISBN 0-13-549758-2 (pbk.)

A SPECTRUM BOOK

10 9 8 7 6 5 4 3 2 1

Printed in the United States of America

ISBN 0-13-549758-2 {PBK.}

ISBN 0-13-549766-3

Editorial/production supervision by Cyndy Lyle Rymer
Manufacturing buyer Cathie Lenard
Cover design by Hal Siegel

Prentice-Hall International, Inc., *London*
Prentice-Hall of Australia Pty. Limited, *Sydney*
Prentice-Hall of Canada, Inc., *Toronto*
Prentice-Hall of India Private Limited, *New Delhi*
Prentice-Hall of Japan, Inc., *Tokyo*
Prentice-Hall of Southeast Asia Pte. Ltd., *Singapore*
Whitehall Books Limited, *Wellington, New Zealand*
Editora Prentice-Hall do Brasil Ltda., *Rio de Janeiro*

Contents

Preface

Frank J. Derfler, Jr., is a telecommunications manager with the Department of Defense. He has published numerous magazine and journal articles related to technology and computer systems, as well as two books titled *TRS 80 Communication Systems* and *Microcomputer Data Communication* Systems (Prentice Hall/Spectrum Books).

William Stallings is a senior data communications consultant at Honeywell, Inc. He has managed the design and development of several data communication systems and has published many articles. He received his Ph.D. in computer science from M.I.T.

The term *local network* refers to the total electrical system that links computers, data systems, word processors, and other equipment in offices and buildings.

The purpose of this book is to provide business managers and corporate decision makers with the vocabulary and principles of local network systems. It is the book that should be read before an IBM, Wang, or Xerox representative comes to call. It gives the manager tools to evaluate proposals, determine needs, and ask appropriate questions.

This work stresses the practical applications of local networks. It describes the features and applications of local networks in general and the features and terms used in some specific systems. It provides information on methods of evaluating systems and introducing systems into the office environment. Only functional definitions are used. No background in mathematics, electronics, or computer systems is needed to understand the material, but some knowledge of office and business practices is presumed.

This book is primarily aimed at executives in business, government, and education who are interested in improving office productivity and learning about the latest in communications and computing technology.

ACKNOWLEDGMENTS

We thank Gary Moss for his help on the graphics and Zwi Kohorn for his psychological and practical support.

To my wife, Marlene, and my daughter, Shandra.

F.J.D.

To my wife, Tricia.

W.S.

Chapter 1

Business, Communications, and Productivity

The need to communicate in order to manage business affairs developed centuries before the introduction of electrical signaling devices. The prestigious House of Taxis served as messengers for merchants and royalty in Europe for over two centuries.

Throughout history, human messengers operated in three ways: (1) Special messengers carried documents directly between specific offices, (2) generalized carriers transported documents to a central facility where they were sorted and forwarded, and (3) regular messengers traveled a particular route, picking up and delivering messages to various offices as they completed their circular course. The information paths we use today have not changed in pattern from those traveled by generations of human messengers. The humans have been replaced by electrons and the paths are traced in copper wire or even glass fibers, but the concepts and patterns have remained.

Large offices had the need to move information internally before the use of electrical signaling. They hired their own messengers to move information within a building or series of buildings. Now, modern organizations still need to move information internally, but human messengers have become expensive and cannot efficiently handle the packages we put information into today. A corporate executive who asks to see the "files" in a modern organization may be presented with a floppy disk or a microfiche card and magnifying glass. Modern information-storage and manipulation methods must be accompanied by equally modern methods of information movement.

The explosion of information, the use of information-production and information-sorting machines, the low cost of digital systems, and the high cost of people have all combined to produce systems called *local networks*, which move information electrically in an office, building, or complex of buildings. These networks are the key factor in bringing the kind of increase in productivity to office work that the introduction of automatic machines brought to manufacturing.

Between 1968 and 1978, the introduction of digitally controlled production machinery brought an 83-percent increase in the productivity of blue-collar workers in the United States. During the same period, the productivity of white-collar office workers rose just 4 percent. Since that time, the information of office equipment to sort and produce information has started a sharp rise in white-collar productivity, but that rise will stop abruptly if the sorted and generated information cannot be retrieved and distributed efficiently. The efficient movement of office information is critical to the improvement of office productivity.

The first kind of local electronic information-movement system to come into common use was the private branch exchange (PBX) telephone system. The PBX began as a local switchboard that connected office telephones with each other and with outside lines. The manual switchboard system was followed by an automatic version known as the private automatic branch exchange (PABX), which removed the human telephone operator from many functions. In the past, the PABX telephone system was quite separate from any corporate system for computer interconnection, but now modern PABX systems route the digital signals from computers, word processors, and other digital information devices through buildings along with voice telephone calls.

Corporate or institutional computer centers have traditionally been separated from communications functions. Computer centers often came under the authority of financial managers, while communications was a part of corporate operations. When computer centers needed to interconnect to exchange data, they often established dedicated point-to-point circuits using lines leased from the telephone company. In traditional installations, communications between terminals and the host computer are provided on a point-to-point basis using leased lines, dialed calls, or hardwired circuits.

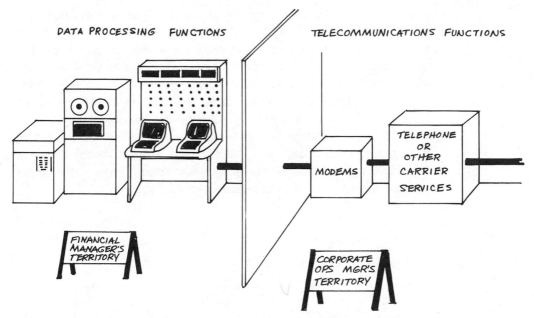

DATA PROCESSING FUNCTIONS

TELECOMMUNICATIONS FUNCTIONS

TELEPHONE
OR
OTHER
CARRIER
SERVICES

MODEMS

FINANCIAL MANAGER'S TERRITORY

CORPORATE OPS MGR'S TERRITORY

Figure 1-1 Typically, corporate data processing and corporate communications have been managed by different functional managers. Technology is rapidly breaking down the wall between these operations.

The traditional point-to-point approach has significant drawbacks. It is very expensive to establish circuits for a large number of interconnections, and the system is inflexible once it is established. Expansion or modification of the system can create large costs that limit a manager's flexibility in restructuring the organization. The corporate organization chart can remain wedded to the computer wiring diagram long after both are obsolete.

Modern interconnection systems must meet the corporate needs for flexibility and capability for expansion. They must meet the technical performance needs of speed and accuracy, and they must face new issues of intrusion resistance and security. The ultimate goal of an interconnection program should be to produce a system that maximizes performance, flexibility, and security while simultaneously minimizing total cost.

LOCAL AREA NETWORKS

Local area networks provide a relatively new alternative to the cumbersome and expensive point-to-point interconnection of office machines and computers. The PABX is one form of local network; others will be defined later. In all local networks, the concept is that of an invisible messenger carrying information from place to place either on request or as a part of a regular routine. The local network strives to eliminate the wasteful reentry of data on the keyboards of many different machines and to make current information available—within the limits of security and privacy—throughout the organization.

The local network consists of several functional elements, which vary greatly in physical form and location. The functional elements include a transmission medium, network control, local attachment points, and interface with the outside world.

TRANSMISSION MEDIA

Most networks currently in use transmit data over coaxial cable or twisted-pair wire cables. Fiber-optic technology is evolving rapidly, and this medium has great potential for meeting applications where very-high-speed data or combined data and video service is needed. Multiconductor copper wire is the simplest medium being used. It can provide moderate-speed service over distances of about 1 kilometer between repeaters (devices that repeat the signal for more strength and clarity).

Coaxial cable is becoming the most commonly used transmission medium. Coaxial cable can provide high-speed data service as well as simultaneous service for voice, music, or video. The experience of the cable television industry has boosted the popularity of coaxial-cable data systems. Connectors and other hardware, installation techniques, and some very practical experience have been borrowed from the cable television industry and used in local networks. In many cases existing cable television installations can be adapted to local network use.

The bandwidth of fiber-optic cables (and therefore their data speed, number of services, and so on) is much higher than that of coaxial cables, and signals can be transmitted for a longer distance without repeaters. The advantages of fiber-optic cables over both copper wire and coaxial cables include high security, freedom from electrical interference, and the elimination of troublesome electrical installation problems.

Transmission Media

- coaxial cable
- fiber optic cable
- twisted pairs

Figure 1-2

Fiber-optic cables may be less expensive than wire or coaxial cable systems in many applications. Two major disadvantages of fiber optics systems are: (1) The need for installers and possibly maintainers with special training, and (2) the inability to support a large number of stations (over fifty) on a network.

NETWORK TOPOLOGY

Topology is an information-industry buzzword that you should learn simply because it is so commonly used. As it is used in the industry, it refers to the physical design or shape of the system. It is the pattern of interconnection used among devices on the network. In general, the topology of a network can be described as a star, ring, or tree. In practice, large networks become a combination of these topologies.

A *star network* resembles a special messenger who goes to a point, makes a pickup, and returns the package to a central distribution warehouse. It consists of a central controlling hub which is connected by a point-to-point communications circuit to every other device on the network. This system is familiar as the type of connection used by traditional large computer installations. The central system can relay information among all of the communicating terminals quite well, but it may not be cost effective to have a powerful central system serve in a relay role. If the central controller stops working, the entire network stops. The high overhead cost and potential vulnerability of the star topology can be disadvantageous. The PABX is a type of star, since it consists of a central switching mechanism, with wires radiating to attached devices.

The *ring, loop,* or *daisy-chain topology* is a pattern of computing elements arranged in a circle. Control can be centralized, by establish-

Topology
(Pattern of Interconnection)

- star
- ring
- tree

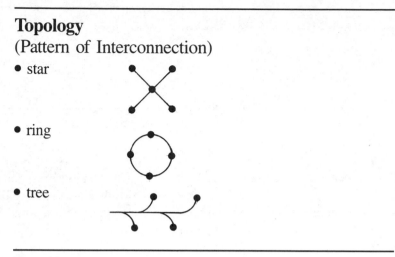

Figure 1-3

ing a primary control note, or distributed, with all nodes having equal status. In the ring network, a message is passed from node to node along unidirectional links until it reaches its destination.

Ring networks make efficient use of the transmission medium and can be used on simple wire systems. However, each element in the ring plays an active role, and the failure of two or more elements can isolate sections of the ring.

The *bus* or *tree topology* arranges the elements of the system like the leaves on a tree. The communicating devices share the "bus," or transmission medium.

In the bus network, a message from the originating node is broadcast along the bus to all other attached devices. The destination node reads the message as it goes by. When the transmission medium is a cable (coaxial, fiber-optic, or wire ribbon), this is commonly called a *cable-bus network*.

Bus networks are quite suitable for serving many users at a single site where the longest distance between users is a few kilometers. Filtering repeaters can be installed in some bus networks to link local systems over greater distances. Certain types of cable-bus systems with large capacities may carry different services (data, voice, and video) on the same cable.

A MANAGER'S CONSIDERATIONS

Electrical interconnection systems can vary in many technical ways: medium, topology, data rate, types of services, and so on. But users of these systems are more concerned with considerations such as performance, flexibility, security, and cost. The following chapters describe more of the technical differences in interconnection systems and will help you to develop the ability to assess various systems according to your needs.

Chapter 2

Communicating Office Machines

Just a few years ago, an automated office was one that had a few electric typewriters on various desks and a photocopy machine in the corner. The number of devices in most offices has increased to include word processing machines, electronic display typewriters, and fac-simile machines. But in many otherwise modern offices, accounting computers are still completely separate devices and telephone manage-ment is done by little more than personal whim. The net result of almost all efforts in today's office is still information printed on paper.

Paper has certainly served us well. It is a medium of information transportation that is easy to use. It is relatively effective and cheap. If kept from fire, water, and excessive sunlight, paper documents can last for hundreds of years. Large office files can become bulky, but various administrative actions, such as adding a file room, can take care of the storage problem. Transporting information on paper is the way we have done things for hundreds of years, and we are comfortable with it.

INFORMATION ON PAPER

But moving information on paper can also be a very labor-intensive business. The information on the paper is not easily changed or rearranged except by cutting and pasting the paper itself. U.S.

Department of Labor studies show that over 50 percent of the work force of the average American industry is involved in various forms of paper handling. More than 85 percent of all business communications in the United States is conducted by means of words written on paper. (Some 15 percent of all business letters are written to clarify previously written letters that were unclear.) Indeed, over 52 percent of the gross national product of the United States comes from what is broadly called the "information industry." If the information produced by this huge industry is all going to move on paper, timberland should be the investment of the century!

Most of the office machines in use today are designed to print on, copy, bind, move, or otherwise process the paper that carries information. Except for such innovations as the office copier (main function: to make more paper), little has changed in the way most offices do their work in the last thirty years. We give a great deal of attention to paper because, in many cases, the medium is a large part of the message we send.

Figure 2-1 This demonstration of an electronic office uses Honeywell equipment to develop and distribute information through the use of shared large-memory storage devices. (Photo courtesy of the Honeywell Corporation.)

The term *paperless office* has become very popular. This concept is probably acceptable as a goal, but for most of us, the end products of our office work will still be transported on paper for many years—and that isn't bad. Paper is very portable and can present graphics and words in an effective way and at a price that the electronic media cannot match. But as a manager you have to ask, "Even if my end product is printed on paper, isn't there some way to improve the process of developing that product?"

PAPER AND PRODUCTIVITY

Productivity in the office environment has received major attention only in the last few years. Productivity can be (and usually is) measured by such factors as the number of pages produced or the speed with which a document is prepared. Since quality is a much more subjective and personal factor, efforts to improve the quality of the productive work in an office are difficult to measure and vulnerable to strong resistance at many levels. But there can be little real argument about objective quantity measures of productivity. There are figures showing the benefit of some investment in terms of an increase in office productivity, but charts showing an increase in quality are very hard to make. For that reason, the next few pages will treat quantity of work as if it were the major factor in office productivity. Later chapters will deal with improving the quality of work through the efficient transfer of information.

WORD PROCESSORS:
Paper In, Paper Out

After an office copier, the first device a manager thinks about to help produce the information-on-paper that is the final product of his office is a word processor. A *word processor* is a special-purpose computer that substitutes a video screen or other electronic display for paper. Some units go so far with this substitution theme that the data on the screen moves about and is treated just like a piece of paper in a typewriter. Everything is typed on a line that simulates the platen of a typewriter, and each document is filed page by page.

Figure 2-2 An electronic word processor is actually a device for transferring information from one kind, quality, size, or shape of paper to another. Providing a word processor with an electronic communications capability can break the paper chain.

Word processors (and the operators who use them) are often used as paper-transformation devices. Paper is put into the system in the form of drafts and notes, and paper comes out in the form of a more or less finished product. In most cases, the documents and drafts must be entered into the machine from the keyboard. This is a lengthy process, subject to error, which often duplicates the keyboard entries of someone else somewhere else. Often the raw material we feed into the word processor was created on a keyboard in our own company or office. Doesn't it make sense to keyboard the information only once and save the additional time, energy, and correction effort? Of course it does! If only the process of transferring information were as simple as it looked.

FLOPPIES, TAPES, CARTRIDGES ...

Word processors store the documents they create on some kind of electronic medium. The older IBM MTST devices used cartridges of magnetic tape. Operators had to search along the length of the tape for the document they wanted to recall. The slightly newer "mag card" systems used cards that worked in a manner very similar to the magnetic tape, only the cards could be filed, retrieved, and sorted more easily than the tapes. More modern machines use rotating disks that are also magnetic recording devices. Because of their design, they provide essentially random access to the data they hold. These disks, which are either 8 inches or 5¼ inches in diameter, are referred to as *floppy disks*. (The smaller disks are sometimes called "minifloppies.")

This storage medium would seem to be a simple and easy way to transfer information from one word processing machine to another without the need for rekeyboarding or putting words on paper as an intermediate step. Unfortunately, floppy disks are sort of like the doors on Ford and Chevrolet automobiles; they all serve the same function, operate on the same principles, and look a lot alike, but they are not interchangeable. Word processing machines from different companies will almost never record information on a disk in the same way. Even different models of systems from the same company may not produce interchangeable disks. This very often leads to a situation where complete documents have to be reentered when they were created on a machine only a wall away.

LEGISLATING COMMONALITY

One way around this problem is administratively to direct that all word processing devices in use in a particular company or office have a common disk format. This kind of direction is difficult to enforce, because no single system will meet the needs of all users in any organization. There will always be unique needs that can be defended as exceptions to the rule—and soon exceptions will be the rule.

Some companies have recognized that disk incompatibilities are a way of life and have developed special devices to transform disks from one format to another. This kind of device is priced just under $20,000. Each kind of disk conversion to be done (CPT to Xerox, IBM to Wang, and so on) may require a separate program. This is an expensive way around the problem, but it becomes more economical if several machines that must exchange data on a regular basis are involved.

THE DATA COMMUNICATIONS PORT

There is another electronic way to move information from one word processing machine to another. Most word processing systems have an optional data communications port available. This port can be used to turn the word processing computer into a terminal for another larger computer system. It can also be used to exchange files of documents with other word processing systems.

These data communications ports almost provide the ideal means for transferring information. Their electrical characteristics (described in more detail in chapter 5) meet very specific international standards of compatibility. Given the proper wiring harness and operating programs, the communications ports of most word processors can be used to transmit documents from one system to another without regard for the disk size or format used in recording. Problems, however, still remain. Each system uses unique internal codes—often called control codes—which perform such functions as formatting the document for the printer, keeping margins, and paragraphing. These codes are not standard among systems, so documents transferred through the data communications ports may need extensive reworking before they can be used. Even recognizing the need for possible reworking, the direct transmission of data from one word processor to another can substantially decrease the time a secretary invests at a keyboard to produce information on paper. Decreased production time is one measure of increased productivity in the office environment.

Figure 2-3 The Datapoint 8600 is a device that can serve as a member of the local network or as a stand-alone data processing device. (Photo courtesy of the Datapoint Corporation.)

ACCOUNTING COMPUTERS

The accounting or bookkeeping department is an important part of any office environment. A great deal of information (usually on paper) flows into this department, and a great number of checks and reports (on paper) flow out. Most modern businesses have recognized the benefits of doing payroll, accounts payable, and accounts receivable on a centralized computer system. The care and feeding of this computer system often dominates the operation of the office. The productivity of an accounting office is more often measured by time than by volume. Checks and operating reports have definite schedules that must be met.

Operating reports and business analysis reports often require words to explain their numbers. Word processors are usually used to provide the words. The numbers from the accounting computer are either entered into the word processor (a very tedious process subject to error) or the output sheets from the accounting computer are attached at the back of the introductory comments. Neither process is satisfactory. It would be much easier if the accounting computer could communicate with the word processor and provide it with the numbers that need to be an integral part of the report.

Communication between two machines such as a word processor and an accounting computer is simple in concept. The accounting computer manipulates the information in its memory and files and creates a report full of numbers. Instead of being sent to a printer to be put on paper, these final tables of numbers are sent to the word processor to be stored and then called out as needed for incorporation into the text. The process is made complex by such factors as the electrical signaling and coding standards used, the distances between the machines, and the wiring or cabling needed to connect the machines.

The selection of a proper local network to connect word processors and accounting machines can speed the production of reports and make the distribution of financial data a much simpler task.

FACSIMILE: FRIEND OR FOE?

Many companies have discovered the advantages of using *facsimile* machines to transmit information between widely separated offices ("widely" in this case means anything from one block away to the other side of the world). Facsimile has many advantages over other forms of message transmission. First, it is very flexible. Facsimile can transmit pictures, graphs, drawings, handwritten notes, and anything else that can be put on paper. Second, it saves preparation time because information does not have to be entered into a message system again through a keyboard. The paper itself is scanned for patterns of light and dark, which are transmitted to the receiving end. Until recently, however, facsimile has been a highly paper-oriented transmission media. It took paper in and spit paper out at the other end of a telephone line. The emphasis was not on the information the paper was transporting but on the paper itself. Now, digital facsimile machines that have a capability to communicate with other local office machines are entering the market.

Figure 2-4 The Wang Image Transfer System digitizes the image contained on a piece of paper and transmits it through a network to other Wang systems. The Image Transfer System can scan and digitize text, data, charts, signed forms, and even hand-drawn pictures and notes. (Photo courtesy of Wang Laboratories, Inc.)

Digitizing a page of information allows it to be easily manipulated by computer systems, stored on magnetic disks or tapes, and encrypted for security. In digital form, the pages created by a word processor can be transmitted to a facsimile machine without ever going through the on-paper stage. The transmitting word processor can send the document directly to the receiving facsimile machine using a standard digital transmission format. This capability simplifies the information-movement process and allows one terminal (a facsimile machine) in a distant office to perform several functions.

The more sophisticated of these devices are combined text-graphic systems: Not only can they store, communicate, and render on paper any graphic image, but they also incorporate text-handling capability. Thus, the user can easily create and edit text, combine it with charts, pictures, and other graphics, and subsequently treat the whole thing as an electronic or paper image.

TELEX AND TWX

Another kind of paper producer, the *electronic teleprinter* connected to a Western Union telex or TWX network, is commonly found in many offices. Telex message service is popular because it is economical and fast. But in many offices the economies and speed end right at the teleprinter itself. Telex messages normally appear on paper. This paper is often routed through the office distribution system by administrative clerks. The office distribution system involves "buck-slips," "holy Joe" envelopes (inter-office memos and messenger envelopes), and its own petty bureaucracies. You will probably consider yourself fortunate to receive a teleprinter message on your desk on the same day it entered the building. Lecturers talking about office distribution systems often say that transmitting a message electronically over 3000 miles takes about one minute, whereas moving it the last 100 yards from the teleprinter to the desk of the person to whom it is addressed may take from four hours to a day. The immediacy, impact, and probably some of the increased cost of electrical transmission over standard surface mail has been wasted by an antiquated distribution system designed to handle only information carried on paper.

Many word processors now have the capability to serve as Telex terminals. The terminal program can operate in what is called a *background mode*. This means that the program is operating invisibly in the background while the system performs its normal word processing tasks. A small adapter box usually signals when a Telex message has been received, and the message can be found waiting patiently on a disk file. It can be electronically routed from this file to another word processor, to a printer, or to another office device such as an electrically connected intelligent copy machine.

THE INTELLIGENT COPIER

Another device that can operate without a paper input is the *office copier*. Initially, that statement sounds illogical. A copier must have something to copy, so how can it work without paper? The copier does indeed need something to copy, but the image it copies onto paper can be delivered and stored electronically. Several companies now market intelligent copiers that can receive electronic images of the documents they are to print from word processing, facsimile, accounting, and communications systems and print those images in collated, stapled, stuffed, and addressed form. The intelligent copier can also automatically insert labels, shading, and blank forms that overlay the information to be copied. The user has a choice of type styles and sizes and, in some cases, paper sizes. The intelligent copier is probably going to be the output port of the office of the near future. It will be at this point that information will finally be put onto paper for movement into the public or into other commercial firms. Paper is still one of the best information-movement devices we have—outside the office.

PAPERLESS COMMUNICATIONS

There are two forms of paperless communications which can be found in modern offices. One is extremely common; the other is quite uncommon.

The Telephone

Where would business be without the telephone? Each year corporations pay out millions of dollars in long-distance telephone calls. Even a company with as few as fifty employees can easily spend $3,000 per month on long-distance tolls alone. Reliable studies show that the average successful business call lasts from seven to nine minutes and costs about $3. However, these same studies show that only about 28 percent (some say as low as 15 percent) of business calls are successful. Most callers find that the person with whom they want to talk is out, at a meeting, on another line, or otherwise unavailable. Executives (and their secretaries, who place and filter calls for them) often play extensive and exasperating games of "telephone tag." Each executive takes turns being "it" and having the responsibility to return the call until both players eventually get together. This situation is the direct result of a telecommunications system that has no storage capability. The telecommunications system imposes a kind of tyranny of time on its users. If you want to get information into or out of the telephone network, you have to be ready to receive a call when it comes in or be fortunate enough to find the party you are calling ready to talk. Various devices are now becoming popular that break this time tyranny of telecommunications. Telephone-answering machines and commercial telephone-message storage devices are popular with small businesses, but larger corporations still prefer to give their telephone callers personal (and expensive!) service.

Figure 2-5 The telephone is sometimes not a very accurate way to move information, either!

Some businesses are now providing digital electronic message systems for their customers and executives who have standard computer terminals. These messages are usually text, commonly referred to as *electronic mail,* but can also be audio messages—a reproduction of the sender's vocal message—sometimes referred to as *voicegrams.* Messages can be entered into electronic mail systems, and replies can be made in a prompt, but not necessarily real-time, manner. Digital electronic message systems receive, store, and transmit messages for their users. They can save time wasted on unsuccessful phone calls. They can eliminate the interruptions caused by the telephone. They can also eliminate some of the time office workers spend on administrative filing tasks.

The voice telephone will be an important part of business communications for many years to come, but it will become a smaller part of the total telecommunications system used by businesses. A growing means of providing information will be through the use of video systems.

Video Systems

Video systems used by businesses take many forms. They include the video surveillance and security systems that are so common, video conferencing facilities that seem to have great potential, and executive information stations that are a unique blend of video and computer-graphics techniques.

Video systems must be divided into two types: those that use computer-generated graphics displays and those that display video pictures similar to those seen on commercial television.

Figure 2-6

Video Systems

- Computer generated graphics
- Digital
- Television techniques
- Analog

The growing quality of computer-generated displays makes them appear similar to television pictures, but there are several differences.

Figure 2-7 This is a photograph of the screen of a computer-produced graphics display using teletext technology. This type of display can be transmitted over common telephone lines or digital circuits. It conveys information clearly but lacks rapid animation.

Computer-generated graphics displays transmitted over a local network can use a technology, developed in several countries, called *videotext*. This technology makes use of character generators in the video terminals which are preprogrammed with variable graphics blocks. These graphics blocks can be called and displayed in response to commands received over the communications channel. The resulting pictures are often in multiple colors, but they have only limited animation. They are the result of reasonably intensive programming efforts, and while they can transmit a great deal of information to the user, they are not "live" or even "near real time" displays. The great advantage of computer-generated displays is that they can be sent over any form of local network, dial telephone line, or dedicated cable.

Slow-scan video pictures present a compromise between computer-generated video pictures and full-motion television. Slow-scan video pictures take an average of eight seconds to appear on the screen and they can be changed quickly. They are live, but not full-motion. They are always black and white. Slow-scan video pictures are the result of a scanning process that converts the image of the object into audio tones representing the timing and intensity of the scanning beam.

These audio tones can be transmitted over telephone systems or digitized for transmission over digital networks.

Full-motion video (television) systems have one major characteristic that makes them difficult to use: They require great *bandwidth*. This technical term essentially means that video signals are made up of many frequencies and that they require special high-capacity transmission facilities to carry the picture. The coaxial cable or microwave circuits required to carry one full-motion video picture could carry dozens of simultaneous voice conversations. However, this disadvantage can become an advantage to the executive looking for a way to move large amounts of digital and voice information. If cable facilities are installed to carry full-motion video circuits, they also have ample capacity available to carry some very-high-speed data circuits and digitized voice channels. Of course, new equipment will be required to put the data or voice on the cable, but the expensive and disruptive job of installing coaxial cable can serve dual or even triple purposes.

VIDEO INFORMATION SYSTEMS

Video-based executive information systems have gained a great deal of popularity in large corporations. In practice, they consist of television sets installed in executive offices and conference rooms. The television system may carry as many as twenty or thirty channels of information. A *TV menu* informs the users of what information is on what channel. The video program on any one channel can come from many different sources. Computer-generated graphics and full-motion video can be fed into different channels on the system.

Some executives find a view from the security-surveillance cameras to be very valuable. By viewing the parking lot, for instance, they can see the effect of weather on their personnel. Daily graphs showing portions of the operating report can be developed from computer graphics displays using current data from the accounting computer. Briefings and business presentations can be placed on videotape and played at the convenience of the individual executives.

These video-based information systems have several advantages over simple computerized executive work stations. The primary advantage is that the information is "prefiltered." A small staff works with the executives to determine exactly what information they want to see and what format they want to see it in. The executives do not have to master computer codes, suffer from program halts, or master a keyboard to obtain the information they want (this last point is a major factor in executive resistance to interactive information systems). A secondary advantage is that executives are not responsible for the accuracy of the information they call up. If they called their own displays on a terminal, they might have to check them for accuracy. If the information is presented to them, others are responsible for the accuracy of the information.

Video conferencing is also a technique that promises to become a cost-effective means for increasing executive productivity. Video conferences can be held with participants who are thousands of feet or thousands of miles apart. Satellite links are usually used to bring in video from hundreds or thousands of miles away, but broadband local networks can be used to distribute the conference video locally and to link corporate facilities.

The great potential for video displays of information extends beyond the executive suite. Any person who has traveled through a major airport knows the value of television monitors in providing complete and current information. Manufacturing and service organizations could also benefit from the use of video status boards that provide current information to all corners of the organization.

THINGS TO THINK ABOUT

Anyone considering a method of information distribution in an office or place of business must consider many factors. These include:

- The fact that information on paper will continue to be an end product of offices for many years to come. But it does not have to be an interim waste product too!
- The fact that various departments, such as accounting, administration, and publications, are valuable sources of information that should be shared throughout the organization.
- The importance of modern products such as intelligent copiers, digital facsimile machines, and communicating word processors.
- The positive and negative aspects of voice telephone systems.
- The future need for and value of video information systems.

These factors are only the first of a long list of practical, technical, and psychological considerations we will examine. The next chapter deals more with the technology of information distribution systems.

Chapter 3

Modern Information Movement Systems

Chapters 3 and 4 describe some of the technical aspects of the various kinds of interconnection systems that can be used to transport information from place to place in an office, business, institution, or factory. Our purpose is to show you what is practical and important and to acquaint you with some of the buzzwords of the industry so that you can hold your head above water in meetings with salespeople and consultants. We begin with the most common type of interconnection device: the existing telephone system.

PBX AND PABX

Almost all businesses have found some sort of in-house telephone system to be a necessity. This telephone system may be leased from the local telephone company or other supplier, or it may be purchased outright. Usually, the system also serves as a portal to the outside telephone network, thereby making efficient use of local telephone trunk lines and special leased circuits, WATS lines, or the services of alternative telephone carriers. The earliest form of local service was the *private branch exchange (PBX),* typified by a company telephone operator sitting in front of a large plugboard, inserting jacks and responding to flashing lights. The next step in the development of

Figure 3-1 A private automatic branch exchange (PABX) performs many line-switching functions without the aid of an operator.

telephone systems was the *private automatic branch exchange (PABX)*, which provided a self-dialing capability for system users, enabling them to place their own calls without operator intervention. Operators are still often used to screen incoming calls, but their workload is greatly reduced, and they may double as office receptionists.

In 1968, the U.S. Supreme Court handed down the famous Carterfone decision which allowed companies other than the telephone companies to provide equipment that attached to telephone company lines. Electronics and communications firms then began a competitive race to provide the most features and greatest flexibility in the PABX market. Features such as call forwarding, call waiting, and many others came into common use. The introduction of computer power into the PABX allowed it to keep accurate records of calls made and logically to choose the least expensive routing for a call. The most modern PABXs—now variously called computer branch exchanges (CBX), electronic private branch exchanges (EPBX), integrated computer-based branch exchanges (ICBX), telephone controllers, and many others—can provide extensive reports on telephone usage. They can

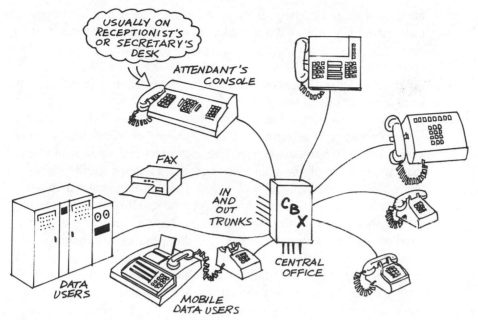

USUALLY ON RECEPTIONIST'S OR SECRETARY'S DESK

ATTENDANT'S CONSOLE

FAX

IN AND OUT TRUNKS

CBX

CENTRAL OFFICE

DATA USERS

MOBILE DATA USERS

Figure 3-2 A computer branch exchange can use various techniques to integrate voice and digital data on the same system.

quickly reconfigure their internal switching scheme to inexpensively keep up with business reorganizations or the creation of temporary task groups. Remember, no matter what they call them, the "BX" kinds of equipment are essentially centralized switching systems that have grown from private voice-telephone installations.

The presence of these PABX devices in almost every modern office means that each office has wiring installed which runs to a central point. This wiring represents a large investment in the communications and information-movement capabilities of the company. This existing wiring plant is a very attractive way to move digital electronic information along with the voice traffic it now carries. Indeed, several companies have introduced combined data-and voice-switching PABXs.

VOICE AND DATA PABX

A combined voice-data PABX (which may be called a CBX, ICBX, and so on) is one that makes dual use of the switching circuits and building wiring to carry both kinds of information. Combined systems may restrict where digital terminals are located and limit some of their capabilities, or they may be very flexible in the way voice and data systems can be mixed. But the combined data-voice PABX must be given serious consideration for anyone interested in the benefits of local information networks.

In its most simple form, a combined voice-data PABX is created by connecting a data terminal to a telephone line. The data terminal uses a device called a *modem* to change its electrical signals into tones that can travel over the telephone circuits. Modems are available in many shapes and sizes and with many different technical characteristics. Some modems are portable and can be used by simply inserting the telephone handset into rubber cups that hold it securely over a small speaker and microphone. Tones are then exchanged between the modem and the telephone handset. This form of connection is called *acoustic coupling*. Other modems connect directly to the telephone lines. All modems connect directly to the terminal or computer they serve by a fairly short (20-meter maximum) electrical cable.

Essentially, you should remember that modems are devices that convert the local direct current signals used by terminals and com-

Figure 3-3 Figure 3-4 Modems are used to translate between the kind of electrical signals used by computers and terminals and the kind of signals which can be sent over telephone lines. The Prentice Star modem is a semi-portable device that uses an acoustical coupler to connect to the telephone lines. The Prentice P 212C is a more sophisticated device containing a microprocessor which is capable of operation at higher speeds.

puters into another form (usually analog signals representing audio tones) which can be sent longer distances without degradation. The data rate on this kind of system is limited by the bandwidth of the telephone lines and by noise introduced into the circuits by the switching equipment. Normally, the data rate used would not be over 4800 bits per second. Some specially conditioned circuits may carry data at speeds of up to 9600 bits per second. (Bits per second and other measures of transmission speed are explained under "Bits and Bauds" later in this chapter.)

Other kinds of modems are used for other kinds of transmission systems. Radio frequency (RF) modems are used to convert the direct-current signals from a computer or terminal into radio signals that can be sent over coaxial cable or out into free space as radio waves. Fiber-optic modems convert the signals into light which can ride a plastic or glass lightwave pipe.

Integrating Data into the PABX

In the next evolutionary step, several manufacturers recognized the need for a data communications capability in the PABX systems and made some special options available. The SL-1 PABX system from Northern Telecom allows users to continue a normal voice conversation while sending data over the same telephone wire. This advancement helped to integrate digital systems into the analog voice network, but it was only a stopgap measure. A revolutionary branching was needed in the PABX evolutionary tree.

The Digital PABX

There are different ways of putting together a modern voice-digital PABX. The most technically sophisticated is the all-digital system.

The *all-digital PABX* turns the old system on its head. Instead of trying to integrate digital computers and terminals into a voice system, the new systems are optimized for the transmission of data signals. In this new architecture, electronic circuitry converts the audio sounds from telephones into digital signals. The circuitry to do this may be contained at a central location or in the telephone, but the point is that the analog voice signals are converted to digital bits for routing and switching. The conversion of voice to digital signals is certainly more expensive than using only standard voice instruments, but the use of all-digital circuitry allows computers and terminals to exchange information at high speed with low noise. Furthermore, since the

Figure 3-5 This illustration shows the Information Switching Exchange (ISX) marketed by Datapoint Corporation. It is a digital PBX that utilizes dispersed switching technology to integrate voice, data, text, electronic message services, and Datapoint's ARC coaxial-cable local network. The system allows for phased growth from 100 to over 20,000 voice and data stations.

Voice communications will remain an important part of the office of the future. Managers considering information-movement needs should become familiar with the many voice storage, recognition, and synthesis systems becoming available. People were born to listen and talk. Voice is the natural form of communications, and managers should consider voice needs. (Photo courtesy of Datapoint Corporation.)

automated devices may now send digital signals into the PABX, the need for modems is eliminated. In an all-digital PABX, voice data and computer data both use the same system in a highly efficient manner.

Another, slightly less integrated approach is that of a hybrid *office controller* system. This kind of hybrid system may split the digital signals and analog voice signals into two groups for the purposes of

Figure 3-6 While technically not a local network, MICOM's Micro600 Port Controller is a very versatile device that allows communications among many different kinds of digital systems and devices. The Port Selector is installed between the main computer and the using terminals to provide first-come, first-served access and communications to remote devices. This allows terminal connections to be made for only the period of time they are needed and insures that connections are made in the most cost-effective manner. (Photo courtesy of MICOM Systems, Inc.)

local switching. This avoids most of the costs of converting voices to digital signals and back again. The two signal groups interface, however, through the PABX, which still routes, switches, regulates, and records connections with the communications systems outside the local network.

All routing and switching in a digital private branch exchange are done by the central logic unit or central switch. Very large installations may have subswitches, which take some of the load off the central switch and limit the need for expensive interbuilding cabling.

A centralized digital PABX is a high-technology device that has one major drawback: If the central system malfunctions, all electronic communications stop. Since it is a computerized system, it will suffer from malfunctions. Of course, modern systems are built in a modular fashion with redundant and easily replaced parts, but unless you are

Figure 3-7 The Wang Audio Workstation provides voice and data inputs into the Wang Alliance Office System. Voice documents can be created through the Audio Workstation, which has a digital-based voice editor that allows authors to dictate, review, and edit voice documents. The work station can also route voicegram messages, through an automatic dialing function, to other Audio Workstation users. (Photo courtesy of Wang Laboratories, Inc.)

completely immune from Murphy's Law ("If anything can go wrong, it will"), you have to assign some weight to the vulnerability of a combined voice and data system when you make decisions about system selection. Also, PBX systems cannot switch or carry full-motion video information systems.

This look at using the PABX to transport digital information has only described the systems and divided them according to how they operate. Before we move on to the next kind of local connection scheme, the all-digital communications bus, we have to get some technical talk out of the way. Consider the following paragraphs on data transmission speed and signaling as a vocabulary builder. You need to speak the language before you can make a decision on the kind of system that will best suit your needs.

FULL- AND HALF-DUPLEX MODEMS

The term *full-duplex (FDX)* usually means that data can be sent and received simultaneously by a data communications device. In modems, that is exactly what the term means. The terms *full-* and *half-duplex* take on a slightly different meaning in reference to terminals, and we will discuss this shortly.

With modems, *full-duplex* means simultaneous bidirectional communications using two sets of modem tones (audio modems) or two sets of frequencies (RF modems). The use of two pairs of frequencies allows each modem to transmit and receive at the same time. This uses up a great deal of the available communications channel and is usually used at lower speeds.

Half-duplex modems can only transmit or listen; they cannot do both at the same time. This is similar to ham radio or police radio transmissions where each operator says "over" at the end of each transmission to signal that the channel is clear. Half-duplex operation requires that the modems and computers recognize when the line is clear. Some modems may use a very-slow-speed *back channel* which signals that the receiving modem wants to send. This back channel is used to coordinate what is called the *turnaround* when one modem stops transmission and the other begins.

TELEPHONE MODEMS

Telephone modems are relatively simple devices that are shrouded in technical and proprietary marketing terms. They are, for instance, called *data sets* by many telephone companies. In some smaller telephone companies, it may be difficult to find many marketing people who understand either data sets or modems.

All data systems communicating over telephone lines need a *modulator-dem*odulator, or *modem,* to link the telephone lines to the computer or terminal. The modem modulates and demodulates audio tones transmitted over the telephone circuits. The telephone system of the 1980s is designed to carry only audio signals in the form of alternating-current voltages. Computers and terminals transmit information in the form of digitally coded direct-current voltages. At some time in the future, all communications systems may be digital and the telephone systems may accept direct-current pulses from homes and offices, but until that time we must feed sounds converted into analog voltages, not DC pulses, down the telephone lines. A modem sends and receives analog signals or audio tones over the telephone line on one end and direct-current digital pulses for computers and terminals on the other end. The electronic components within the modem manufacture sound in response to digital voltage and digital voltage in response to sound.

Figure 3-8 Even relatively low-cost devices such as personal computers can communicate over telephone lines. This Apple II microcomputer contains a sophisticated modem from the Novation Company which gives it powerful communications capabilities.

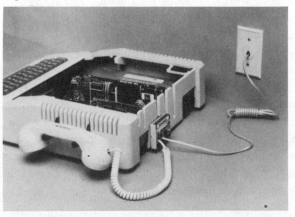

Signaling by Sound

The digital-voltage signaling standard between the modem and the computer or terminal is normally based on the EIA standard RS-232-C. The frequencies of the tones used over the telephone lines are determined by another standard. The most common tone signaling standard in the United States is the one established by Bell Telephone Laboratories called Bell 103. The Bell 103 standard is used for low-speed modems operating up to 300 baud.

In digital communications, we are only interested in representing the digits zero and one; that is, we need to show two states or conditions only. If we use sound to transmit digital information, we could simply turn the sound off and on to represent 0 and 1, but this off-on signaling would leave room for error. The absence of sound might be a correct signal, but it might also be a broken connection or an interruption by noise. Two-tone signaling was adopted to represent digital information on audio systems. With two tones, we know that if tone A is not present, tone B should be. If neither tone is there, the system can immediately detect a problem.

In the Bell 103 standard, the station originating the call (usually thought of as a terminal) uses a tone of 2225 Hz to represent a 1 and of 2025 Hz to represent a 0. Obviously, if the modem at the answering end transmits back with the same two tones, only one side of the conversation will be able to "talk" at a time. If, however, the answering equipment uses two different tones, then we can use selective filters to detect only the desired signals, and a simultaneous two-way conversation can take place. Simultaneous two-way transmissions over telephone lines is referred to as *full-duplex transmission*. Most modems (and all the low-speed modems commonly used in electronic message systems) use four tones for signaling, two on the originating side and two on the answering side. The Bell 103 standards are:

Type	Logic	RS-232-C Voltage	Tone
Originate	1	−3 to −24 volts	2225Hz
Originate	0	+3 to +24 volts	2025Hz
Answer	1	−3 to −24 volts	1270Hz
Answer	0	+3 to +24 volts	1070Hz

The tones listed are those transmitted by each side. A modem transmits one set of tones, but it receives the other. Many kit builders and home designers have forgotten this simple fact and end up only receiving their own tones.

Higher-Speed Transmission

Other modem standards, such as Bell 202, Bell 212, and the signaling tones adopted by companies such as Anderson Jacobson and Racal-Vadic, are commonly found in commercial data communications systems. These modems use various schemes to provide higher signaling rates. The 202-series modems, for instance, are asynchronous devices that can transfer data at a maximum rate of about 1200 bits per second on standard phone lines. But they only transmit in one direction at a time (half-duplex transmission). They use a mark frequency of 1200 Hz and a space frequency of 2200 Hz. Complex "handshaking" signals are exchanged between the modems on each end of the line to control which modem will transmit at any given moment. The 202 signaling path sometimes includes a very slow (perhaps 5-baud) reverse channel over which the nontransmitting modem can signal for attention. This slow-speed channel is used to coordinate channel turnaround.

The 202 signaling system is used commercially in systems where main computers and peripheral devices have lengthy blocks of data to send in one direction. They are commonly used in polling systems in which a computer contacts the peripheral device only periodically.

Bell 212

The more commonly used high-speed transmission method is Bell 212. Bell 212 modems operate in the full-duplex mode, but they do not use frequency-shifted keying. An originate modem operating in the 212 scheme transmits a 1200-Hz tone. The answer modem transmits a 2400-Hz tone. Each tone is shifted in phase instead of in frequency. A digital 1 or 0 transmitted at 1200 baud is only about 0.8 milliseconds long. This is not enough time to detect the frequency of a tone reliably. Changes in phase can be detected by electronic equipment very rapidly, but the phase-detection equipment is more sophisticated than a frequency-discriminating circuit. Phase-shifting modems can transmit data rapidly in full-duplex, but they cost many times more than frequency-shifted devices. A commercial Bell 212 modem will cost between $750 and $1200 dollars. Such modems can be rented from most telephone companies for a monthly fee.

The Bell 212 and Bell 202 standard modems are not compatible with each other. The 212 standard is most commonly used by information utilities, time-sharing services, and other commercial services. The 202 standard is often used by computer systems exchanging data using a polling scheme.

Modems can be an integral part of local networks whenever information has to be sent more than a few hundred feet over twisted-pair cable or whenever a "dial-up" port for interface with the outside telephone lines is desired.

FULL- AND HALF-DUPLEX TERMINALS

The terms *full-* and *half-duplex* take on slightly different meanings when they are associated with terminals or computers acting as terminals. A terminal operating in half-duplex displays its own characters on the screen (or printer) as they are transmitted. A terminal operating in full-duplex (or echoplex, as it is sometimes called) expects to have its transmitted characters echoed back from the distant end (or from its own modem, if the modem is in half-duplex.) In turn, it may echo back characters it receives. A distant end-echo serves as a positive and constant check of the quality of the transmission path.

BITS AND BAUDS

Modems, terminals, computers, and all devices that are digital can operate at various speeds of service. Transmission speeds can be described in four ways. The particular description you use depends on what kind of work you are doing with a data communications or information-transfer system, but you will hear them all at one time or another. You need to know how they relate to each other and to the service they can provide for you. The most common term used in electronic message systems and information utilities is *baud*. The *baud rate* is simply the measure of transmission speed. Baud rate is not the same as bits per second, and the two should not be directly substituted for each other—but they often are. The difference is like describing a stream of water. You can talk about the water moving at so many feet or meters per second or you can talk about so many gallons or liters passing a certain point in a second. They are two different measures of the flowing stream. Baud rate is the equivalent of velocity. Mathematically, it is the reciprocal of the time duration of the shortest signal element in a transmission. A signal element is usually a change in a direct-current electrical potential between high and low voltage or a change in an audio tone between high and low frequency. The time width of one signaling element of information at 300 baud works out to be a little over 3.3 milliseconds. That is about the slowest speed used in commercial computer communications systems. The higher the speed, the shorter each signaling element becomes. That is why high-speed circuits need to be of very high quality. Even a very short burst of noise on the circuit could wipe out a great number of important data bits.

 Bits per second (bps) is a measure of information transfer. It includes only information elements and not other pulses on the line used to introduce or terminate a message. The information element in most systems is either a seven-bit character in the American Standard Code for Information Interchange (ASCII) or an eight-bit character in an IBM developed alphabet called Binary-Coded Decimal Interchange Code (EBCDIC, pronounced eb-see-dick). This is a more practical measure of the information actually getting through a system. Bits per second is directly related to *characters per second (cps)*. What the actual mathematical relationship is depends on the type of system in use, but usually dividing bits per second by 8 will give a useful measure of how many characters per second are coming through a communications circuit. Bits per second or characters per second can also be used to find another common measure of information flow, *words per minute*. Usually, a word consists of six characters (some formulas say five).

The transfer of real information, separated from all of the electrical and administrative bits that various machines and systems require to operate, is referred to as *throughput*. Throughput can be measured in either bits per second, characters per second, or words per minute (wpm).

Typical data rates for terminals operating over telephone lines are 300, 1200, 2400, and sometimes 4800 baud. The price of modems for these various data rates goes up directly with the speed. A person can comfortably read the words appearing on a screen at 300 baud (about 300 wpm). The words appear too quickly to read at 1200 baud, and the information must be presented on a page-by-page basis. Modems running at 300 and 1200 baud can be operated over most normal telephone lines. Higher-speed modems may require special lines, which are also considerably more expensive. Terminals in close proximity to computers and connected directly to them may operate at speeds of up to 9600 baud.

Such speeds are considered slow in terms of computer-to-computer communications. Even speeds of 25,000 bits per second (25 kilobits per second, or 25 kbps) are considered slow by people working with the latest information-transfer systems. Ten million bits per second (10 Mbps) is a standard rate for several modern networks. That certainly is fast, but speed costs money in both initial equipment and upkeep.

Printers can be rated in many different ways. Slower printers are normally rated in characters per second. The slowest mechanical teleprinters operate at speeds of about 10 cps (slightly faster than a good professional typist). Modern offices should not consider a printer that isn't rated for at least 18 to 20 cps. Printers running at 40 cps are commonly used in word processing systems. Computers that output a great deal of paper may use line printers rated in terms of lines per minute. Speeds of 60 lines per minute (about 160 cps, depending on line length and print spacing) are common. Higher-speed printers that literally shoot the paper out in a steady stream are available. But again, speed costs money in terms of initial equipment costs, maintenance, and paper.

Printers are most commonly rated in terms of throughput because there are frequent halts in the printing while paper is moved. A description of characters per second or words per minute only shows the maximum speed of the printing mechanism. Throughput gives some measure of both printing speed and paper-handling speed. Printers can sometimes be equipped with internal *buffers,* elements of electronic memory that can receive data at full speed from a computer or terminal and hold it while the printer mechanism moves paper or positions the print head. If a buffer is not present, the printer and computer must exchange electrical "handshaking" signals that tell the computer when to send and when to hold data transmission to the printer.

Printers are important because they can serve as the final output device of an information system. But before the information reaches a printer in final form, it must be carried around the system for processing, verification, decision making, and formatting. We have examined one possible means of transportation for these data: the telephone system (PABX and all its forms). Now that we have a few insights into the speed factors in digital transmission, the next chapter will look at the kinds of connecting materials used in other local network systems.

THINGS TO REMEMBER

Here are some important points from this chapter to file away:

- Private automatic branch exchanges (PABXs) are small telephone exchanges used by private businesses and institutions. With the addition of computer power, they are gaining the ability to switch digital communications as well as voice calls.
- Modems translate the low direct-current voltages used in computers and terminals into some other form that can be sent over a telephone line, coaxial cable, or fiber-optic cable.

- Bits per second, baud, characters per second, and words per minute are all measures of speed that are related to one another in fairly simple ways. System statistics are often given in terms of maximum speed. Throughput is a measure of what actually gets through the system, not simply what its maximum capability is.

- Higher speed almost always costs more in terms of both initial equipment investment and upkeep.

Chapter 4

Modern Systems: Connections and Standards

If you are going to make sense out of the various local networking plans, you need to know something about how they hook together and what the strengths and weaknesses of their connection schemes are. In this chapter, we will examine several methods of connecting stations together on a local network.

MEDIA

Here is another vocabulary word for you: *media*. When local network people talk about the media, they don't mean the newspapers and television. Instead they mean the various kinds of transmission media that are used to hook together the equipment connected on a local network. The most commonly used media are coaxial cable, twisted-wire pairs, and fiber-optic lightwave pipe.

The media used to connect a local network should be as reliable, easy to install, easy to maintain, and easy to reconfigure as possible. In the long run, these considerations might outweigh such factors as somewhat higher initial costs for materials or maximum-transmission-speed characteristics. The disruptions caused by reinstallation, update, and repair of some media are very good arguments for doing things right the first time.

39

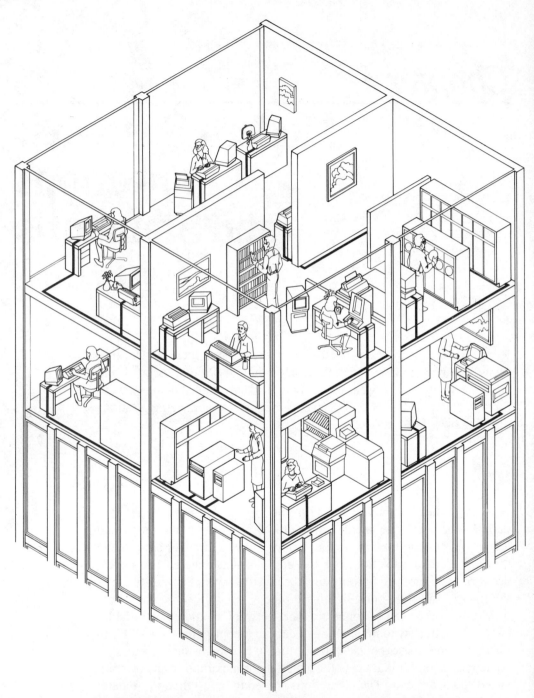

Figure 4-1 This diagram shows conceptually how a bus-type transmission medium can serve many different offices. This cable bus could be either coaxial or fiber-optic. (Diagram courtesy of Xerox Corporation. All rights reserved.)

Most networks currently in use transmit messages over either coaxial cable or twisted pairs of wires. Fiber-optic systems capable of performing very well in specific applications are being offered by several manufacturers.

Twisted Pairs

A twisted pair of copper wires is the simplest form of connection found in modern networks. It is normally easy to install, move, or add to. The cost depends upon the installation method used. If it can be routed internally to the building structure, like telephone wire, the cost is very low. But if local codes or the physical environment requires the use of conduit, it can become very expensive. Twisted pairs have some limitations because signals rapidly lose power as they travel down this kind of connection. It can provide reliable point-to-point communications at speeds of up to 1 megabit per second over a distance of about 1 kilometer. The signal can be extended further through the use of a *repeater,* which regenerates the signal and retransmits it, but the cost of the repeaters can offset the original low cost of the wiring if the data are to be sent any appreciable distance. Remember, the distance to be measured is the actual path of the wire, not a straight line between two

Figure 4-2 Several different kinds of devices are used to connect digital devices to twisted-wire pairs. This device is known as a *line driver*. This is the m-3 asynchronous line driver marketed by bo-sherrel Corp. It draws its power from the unit it is serving and translates the digital signals used in a computer or terminal into a more powerful form that can travel over practical distances without amplifiers or repeaters. Such devices are less expensive than long-distance modems. (Photo courtesy of bo-sherrel Corporation.)

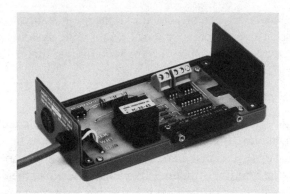

Figure 4-3 This bo-sherrel m-1 short-haul modem performs a function identical to the line driver, but it has its own power supply. Such devices can exchange information over unamplified copper wires for a distance up to 10 miles at slow speeds. The distance of transmission is inversely related to the speed: Thus, a modem like this one can push 9600-baud data 2 miles, 2400-baud data 5 miles, and 600-baud data 10 miles. Two pairs of wires are needed for simultaneous transmission and reception. The modem connects to the RS-232-C port of a terminal or computer. (Photo courtesy of bo-sherrel Corporation.)

Figure 4-4 This bo-sherrel m-4 synchronous short-haul modem is a more sophisticated device that can intercommunicate with two other m-4s at the same time. It can provide a relay function for extended-distance or multiple-station networks. (Photo courtesy of bo-sherrel Corporation.)

points. A twisted pair can travel for 15 feet merely going around a standard doorway. Twisted-pair wiring is susceptible to noise from the environment it passes through. As described earlier, the digital signals are very short in length, and any pulses of electrical noise can result in

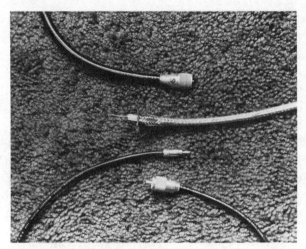

Figure 4-5 This illustration shows the various sizes of coaxial cables and the connectors they come with. The cable in the center has had the outer jacket removed to display the copper shield, central insulating material, and center conductor. These cables would be adequate for baseband systems. Broadband system specifications may call for a double-shielded cable because of the high radio frequencies used.

serious data loss. Twisted pairs should not be routed near heavy-duty electric motors, gasoline engines, welding machines, any other device that sparks, or any device that has a strong electromagnetic field, such as a power transformer or radio transmitter. Twisted-pair connections can be a very valuable low-cost solution for small offices not near industrial operations.

If industrial security is a consideration, twisted-pair wires are a poor choice unless they are enclosed in a protected wire-distribution conduit. Even then, the high-speed signals may actually be radiated by the wires and can be received by sophisticated means some distance from the wires without any physical contact.

Coaxial Cables

The other commonly used form of connection is *coaxial cable*. "Co-ax" is usually made up of one heavy center conductor surrounded by an insulating layer of plastic or plastic foam. A metallic sheath (either braided copper or solid aluminum) is placed over the plastic. The inner conductor and the sheath then share the same common geometric axis and therefore are coaxial to each other (hence the name). The outer sheath is usually covered with another insulated coating. Co-ax comes

43

in standard sizes with outside diameters of about ⅕, ¼, ⅖, and ¾ inches. The size of the co-ax, the type of insulation, and the type of sheath determine how fast and how far signals can travel over the cable.

Different types of coaxial cables are used at various points in a network. Trunk cables are used for long runs between buildings or remote equipment. These are the highest-quality cables, with foam insulation and solid aluminum outer sheaths.

Distribution or *feeder cables* take signals close to the equipment. These are smaller cables, but probably still have solid sheaths. *Drop cables* provide the final link to the equipment and between equipment in a local area. Drop cables are the smallest and most flexible.

Co-ax is not cheap. Material costs alone can easily run $1 per foot. Installation can more than double the price. It isn't easy to install because (particularly in the larger size) it is fairly stiff and cannot make sharp bends. It is best installed in false flooring or ceilings, where it can be easily fed into position. Coaxial cable does not require conduit for installation and can be buried for runs between buildings.

Coaxial cable has a very wide bandwidth. The theoretical transmission speed for coaxial cable is much higher than for twisted pairs. It can easily carry a 10-Mbps data circuit and several channels of video plus many voice conversations at the same time.

The shield on a coaxial cable gives it good resistance to the intrusion of noise. Co-ax is not completely noise-free, but it can provide good service in environments where unshielded wires could not function. It is particularly resistant to electromagnetic interference from sources like radio transmitters.

Coaxial cable provides improved industrial security over twisted-pair wires because it radiates less. It is, however, still easily tapped by anyone who can gain physical access to the cable.

Nothing has helped the popularity of coaxial cable as much as the cable television (CATV) industry. The widespread use of CATV has created a ready supply of cable, parts, and connectors. It has created a pool of persons with knowledge of how cable systems should be installed and maintained. Many buildings are now being wired for CATV during construction, and the executive looking for a local network can often find a very capable high-speed transmission medium already behind the walls.

Fiber-Optic Cable

Both coaxial cable and twisted pairs of wire require that care be taken to insure that they avoid contact with inappropriate electrical grounds.

They must also be routed around heavy manufacturing locations or other sources of interfering noise. Fiber-optic cables do not have these drawbacks. Since fiber-optic cables are made of glass, they are not troubled by the unequal electrical ground potentials often found in large buildings. Lightning and other induced power surges are also not major considerations. Fiber optics have other advantages over copper wire and cables, including potentially lower costs, freedom from tapping and interception, freedom from radio interference, and the elimination of some forms of degradation that take place when electrical signals travel long distances in a conductor.

The potential transmission speed of fiber-optic cables is even higher than that of coaxial cables. Practical fiber-optic systems that can operate at speeds of 20 Mbps over distances of up to 2 kilometers are on the market. The popularity of coaxial cable with CATV companies has probably slowed the development of fiber-optic systems. But CATV companies are also interested in the technology for their heavy-use, short-run requirements. One of the most ambitious projects is installed in London, Ontario. This 322-Mbps system carries twelve color television channels and twelve stereo channels over 8 kilometers. The system electronics were built by Harris Corporation and the ten lengths of six-fiber cable were manufactured by Canstar.

Figure 4-6 Scarcely bigger than an integrated circuit, these Honeywell fiber-optic transmitters and receivers can be mounted on a printed-circuit card and made an integral part of any equipment. They provide very high-quality and high-speed data communications capabilities. (Photo courtesy of Honeywell Corporation.)

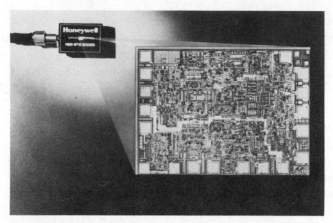

Figure 4-7 The heart of the Honeywell fiber-optic transmitter or receiver is a large-scale integration-technology chip which does the job of converting modulated lightwaves into electrical signals. (Photo courtesy of Honeywell Corporation.)

Fiber-optic installations are still seen less frequently than coaxial-cable installations because of a lack of standardization in the industry and a lack of experience among installers and service organizations. Workers know how to hook up copper wire and co-ax, but coupling optical fibers requires some specialized knowledge. Efficient coupling of the light energy from fiber to fiber and from the fiber cable to the transmitter and receiver requires the use of special connectors and alignment techniques. The lasers and light-emitting diodes used to transmit light down a light pipe are still produced only in small quantities, so their prices are high. Still, fiber-optic technology is rapidly joining with cable and wire systems to deliver information on some other medium than paper.

If you have a very noisy environment, are particularly concerned about security, or have very-high-speed data and video transmission requirements, you should consider fiber-optic cables as an interconnection method. Great potential still exists in the field of fiber optics for development work. Some industries might consider a combination developmental and operational fiber-optic system, which would have unique long-term investment potential.

Pairs of twisted wires, coaxial cables, and fiber-optic cables all have their own specific strengths and weaknesses. They sort themselves out pretty well, depending upon the size of the installation,

Figure 4-8 The Lightlink provides another way to move information using light. The Lightlink transmits, receives, and modulates light beams through the air. The exact distances and speeds that can be used depend upon atmospheric conditions, but Lightlink can be a very economical way to move information between buildings and around buildings without resorting to buried cables or leased circuits.

speed requirements, and conditions of use. Similarly, the ways in which information systems are hooked together can be pretty easily grouped. But beware of anything that appears to allow easy labeling. The practice is often quite different from the preaching!

THE TOPOLOGY

The *topology* of a system refers to the way units in a network are connected together—the geometry of the system. Stations on a network can be strung out like the stops along a bus route, arranged in a circle like the petals of a flower, or laid out like the points of a star. In fact, those are the three common ways of describing the topology of a system: the star, the ring, and the tree.

The Centralized Star Network

A *star network* consists of a central controlling device connected by point-to-point communications circuit to every other device on the network. This is the configuration commonly used to connect a large mainframe computer to its remote terminals. It also describes the layout of most common PABX systems. This pattern permits good communications between the stations on the network and a centralized host. All communications between individual terminals must pass through the host.

This kind of system is particularly appropriate when the host contains all of the data base to be shared or programs to be run. It is, however, a very vulnerable system, because when the host breaks down, all activity stops. A malfunction in the centralized host can disrupt communications between users who really have no need of the host's capabilities other than as a communications relay.

Centralized systems can usually be expanded easily, up to the limit of the central computer's capabilities. The cost to expand beyond that point may be high because it can involve the investment in large hardware packages. Centralized systems can allow easy access into one or more outside communications systems. The central computer can perform all of the functions needed to exchange information with other local or national data networks. Centralized systems can also provide good physical and software security. The central system can be monitored by a human operator who can screen the terminal users desiring access to certain information.

If all of the devices on the system frequently have to exchange a variety of data among themselves, the star can become cumbersome. The centralized computer becomes simply a message switch. It is probably not economical to operate and maintain a large centralized system just to serve as a message switch. In the star network each communications link is exclusively dedicated to the two devices it connects. When these devices are not communicating, the expensive communications link is idle. Even when the units are communicating, their data rates may be considerably less than the capacity of the link,

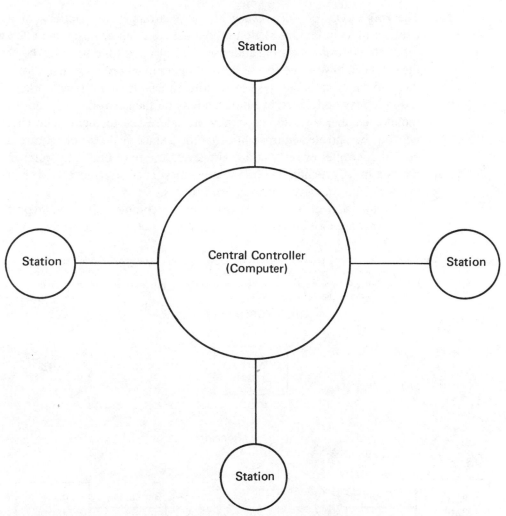

STAR TOPOLOGY

Figure 4-9 The star topology is commonly used when a large central computer-controller is available to perform the functions of switching and controlling the flow of traffic.

particularly if one unit is a terminal and the other a computer. The throughput of a terminal to a computer is probably less than the typing speed of an average typist. It makes little sense to shoot these characters out at a speed of 1200 baud or more when the total throughput is only 60 or 70 cpm in one direction.

49

The Ring Network

The *ring, loop,* or *daisy-chain* topology arranges the stations of a network in a circle. One station on the network can be designated as a master to control the timing and transmissions of all the other units, or the units can have some sort of built-in operational program that allows them to enter into the system at idle times. In a ring network, a message may be relayed by some stations on the network. All stations monitor all messages to see if any are addressed to them. The ring network has greater equipment reliability, since it does not require a central controller or relay point. However, failure of one relay point in the ring may (depending upon the transmission arrangement used) halt the complete message transmission process.

Expansion of a ring network may be complex. It may involve some software or hardware changes in every station. Security in a ring

Figure 4-10 The ring topology depends on active repeaters to relay information around the ring. Any of these repeaters could be the weak link in the system. Despite this, the ring topology has gained acceptance with network developers in Europe. It is becoming more widely accepted in the United States.

RING TOPOLOGY

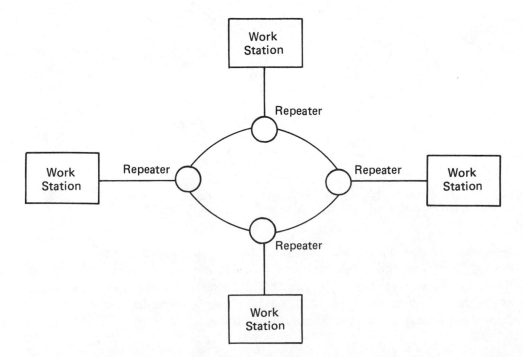

network depends to a large degree on the physical security of the stations themselves.

Ring networks do not lend themselves well to the combination of different kinds of information (video, voice, and data) on the same system.

The Tree or Bus Network

A very common form of interconnection is the *bus* arrangement. On a bus network the stations are attached to a single (or perhaps dual) coaxial or fiber-optic cable. The stations are attached by devices called *cable taps*. The bus system shares several advantages with the ring: (1) It does not require a centralized controller, (2) it does not allow sections

Figure 4-11 This illustration shows the kinds of devices that could be attached to the Ethernet coaxial bus system using a tree topology. Ethernet is a baseband system that is supported by several different manufacturers. (Illustration courtesy of Xerox Corporation. All rights reserved.)

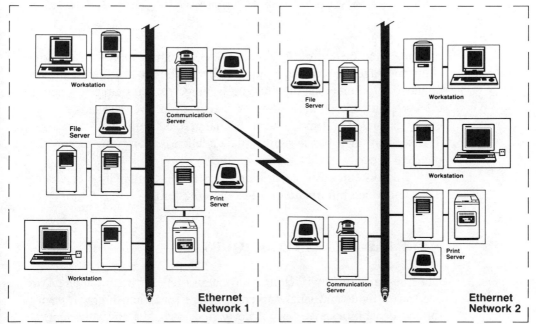

- Multiple Ethernet Inter Connection
- Extended Resource Sharing
- Network Integration
- Multiple Story Office Structure
- Multiple Building Structure
- Remote Office Buildings

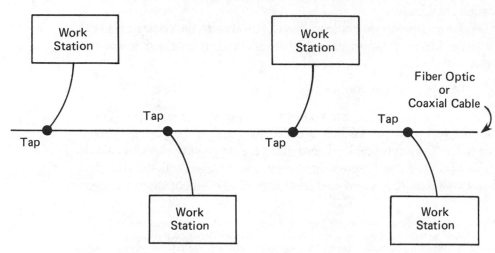

TREE TOPOLOGY

Figure 4-12 The tree topology hangs stations from a common cable bus like leaves from the limb of a tree. Failure of a cable tap will not normally inhibit the operation of the entire system.

of connecting medium to go idle, and (3) it can economically handle short messages exchanged among many different stations. The bus connection scheme has the added advantage of being able to operate effectively if one or more stations malfunction. Bus systems can be easily expanded and modified to exchange data with other networks. The security of a bus system is dependent to a large degree on the physical security of the stations on the system.

Bus systems easily lend themselves to the combination of video, data, and voice information on the same system.

MULTIPLE-ACCESS TECHNIQUES

Our lives are full of written and unwritten rules for getting along. We use traffic lights and lane markers to share roads and highways with limited capabilities. We form orderly lines at banks and supermarket checkout stands to wait for service. Some of the rules we follow are very clear; others depend on many factors that may or may not be operating at the moment. Similarly, stations sharing the same network for the transmission and receipt of information have rules governing how they transmit and receive data. These rules allow multiple users to have access to the information network medium.

Traffic or highways can be divided according to either time or space. Stoplights regulate traffic according to time. Complex switching systems can control several lanes of traffic. Lane markers divide traffic according to space. In some cases lanes are firmly established and in others they are more flexible. Similarly, traffic on an information-movement system can be divided according to time and the electrical equivalent of space: frequency.

Time Sharing

There are several ways in which network stations can share the time available on a system. These include polling, reservation, and contention schemes. Methods of allowing many stations to share the same communications network by regulating the time slots in which they can transmit are called *time-division multiple-access (TDMA) techniques*.

Master-Controlled Methods

Polling is a method of operation found in systems with a master network controller. These are normally large computers operating in

Figure 4-13 Polling is a method of time sharing on a network that relies on a master controller to regulate the transmissions of the network stations.

the star configuration. A polling scheme operates like a good waiter in a restaurant. The server (and the expression "communications server" is actually used in the industry) constantly glances at the customers to see if any need service. When they signal their desires, the server provides a channel of communications. In the meantime, the system keeps busy with housekeeping duties and the needs of the more demanding customers.

Reservation schemes operate, as you might assume, according to a preset schedule. The scheduled transmission time for each station on the network might occur many times a second. If the channel is busy when a station's reservation comes up, the station on the channel will retain priority. Various arrangements prevent stations from making exclusive use of the channel. Reservation schemes usually use a master controller, but this is not an absolute requirement if all stations know exactly what time it is and what the reservation schedule is.

Waiting for the Bus

A method of multiple access known as *contention* is the most widely used on bus-configured networks. Contention schemes operate like automobiles at a four-way stop. The driver arriving at the intersection first proceeds first. If two drivers arrive at exactly the same time, they try and bluff each other out to see who will get across first (they don't know about the rule of yielding right-of-way to the right on the data bus). If both cars start at the same time, they will usually back off until one delays long enough for the other to get through.

We use four-way stop signs at intersections because they are cheaper than stoplights and other forms of controlled access and because they provide an even flow of traffic even if it arrives at the intersection at irregular intervals and in irregular clumps. Stoplights divide the time between roads, but all roads might not have the same amount of traffic. A smart traffic cop could respond to the changing traffic conditions but would be an expensive waste of resources during idle times.

Similarly, the contention scheme has the advantage of being relatively simple yet able to respond to changing traffic patterns on a system. Most bus networks use a contention scheme called *carrier-sense multiple access with collision detection (CSMA/CD)*. Two simple rules of courtesy are used by stations operating on a CSMA/CD contention network: (1) Traffic already in the channel has priority. If a station is transmitting, all other stations just listen. Stations on the network determine if the channel is busy by listening for the radio frequency signal or carrier from another station (the "carrier-sense" portion of CSMA/CD). This technique is really not much more complex than the squelch feature on a citizen's band radio or mobile telephone. (2) If the channel is clear (or when the channel clears), any station may proceed to transmit. If two stations decide to transmit a message at about the same time, they may detect a garble or collision with another message. The affected stations then cut short their transmission and wait a period of time before attempting a retransmission. This is the collision-detection feature of CSMA/CD.

This second rule has a special feature that insures that each station waits a period of time set specifically in its program. This time varies according to the number of failures it has experienced (kind of a frustration level!). This assures that two stations that have collided will not collide again and that one station with the shortest wait time will not monopolize the channel.

CSMA/CD is a very efficient technique. Xerox has proven the system in various operating programs. Published results show that on a network with 120 stations operating under a normal load, stations succeeded in sending their message the first time in over 99 percent of their tries. Stations had to cut their transmissions short and try again only about 0.8 percent of the time.

Figures like these seem to show that collision detection may not be needed in the great majority of transmission attempts. Indeed, some bus networks do not use the collision-detection feature. (They are just called CSMA systems). Each station simply transmits into the network when it has a message. If it does not receive an acknowledgment to its message, it retransmits the message until it does. This system is really more efficient than it seems because of the intermittent nature of data communications systems. It allows the software and equipment to be less complex and allows other manufacturers to avoid the payment of royalties to Xerox for the use of the patented collision-detection techniques.

Catching the Ring

Two sharing schemes are used in ring networks. Both techniques involve passing a signal around and around the ring, either carrying a message or indicating that the network is clear. The first technique is called *slotted ring*. In a slotted ring network, a message called a *frame* is passed from station to station. The frame consists of the leading and trailing information needed for a complete message, but the information elements of the message itself are left blank. A station with a message to transmit fills in the message information as an empty frame goes by. All stations read all frames as they go by. The receiving station removes the message from the frame and sends it on its way. When the original transmitting station receives the frame back again, it knows that the message has been received and marks the frame as empty. This kind of production-line technique assures that timing and spacing of the system are kept constant.

Because of all the frame reading and handling, slotted-ring systems are not very efficient. The transmission speed of the system may be high, but the throughput of the system is low because of all the processing involved.

A more efficient form of message passing frequently used in ring networks is *token passing*. A token consists of a very short message that circulates around the ring, indicating: "The channel is clear." When a station has a message to transmit, it grabs the token and changes it to read: "Here comes a message." The station then transmits a message of any length. After the message is transmitted, the station again changes the token to read: "The channel is clear." Token passing is a popular scheme because it allows stations to pass messages of variable length with little network time needed for management overhead. The token-passing technique may also be used on bus networks with good results.

Frequency Division

The time-division techniques we have just examined are similar to the techniques of using stop signs and stoplights to control highway traffic. Another method used to regulate traffic flow is that of lane markers. Lane markers provide physical separation for cars in ways that are different from the devices that regulate the traffic in time, but both types of separation—time and space—can and are used on the same roadway.

In the same way, both time and space—or either time or space—can be used to regulate traffic on an information-movement network. Information elements can be physically separated by using several different radio (or light) frequencies on the same cable. Just like a radio or television set, the stations on the network are tuned to a specific frequency to transmit and receive their messages.

Baseband vs. Broadband

Network-sharing systems that use only time-division techniques (polling, reservation, slots, tokens, CSMA, or CSMA/CD) are normally called *baseband systems*. The expression refers to the fact that

Figure 4-14 Figure 4-15 These pictures present a front and rear view of the HYPERchannel network adapter marketed by Network Systems Corporation. Their HYPERchannel system uses coaxial-cable trunks to connect various adapters in a baseband network operating at a data rate of 50 Mbps.

Different models of HYPERchannel adapters have been developed to allow equipment from such manufacturers as IBM, CDC, DEC, Honeywell, Burroughs, Cray, Tandem, and Harris to be interconnected on the HYPERchannel network. Each adapter uses a microprocessor to convert and control the communications flow. (Photos courtesy of Network Systems Corporation.)

normally one signal occupies the transmission medium at any one time. Baseband networks are like one-lane roads. The cars traveling down them must take turns using the roadway. Baseband networks can use any form of transmission medium and can be found in any topology.

The alternative to the baseband network is the multilane highway called the *broadband system*. A broadband system allows many different stations to have messages on the network at the same time. The lane markers that divide them are those of frequency. Broadband networks take advantage of the capability of high-quality coaxial cable to carry many different frequencies at one time. These kinds of cables are said to have *wide bandwidth*. The total bandwidth of the cable can be divided among various stations and even among subnetworks in the same way that the commercial radio frequencies are divided between AM broadcast, FM broadcast, television, and so on. Cable systems can carry a radio frequency spectrum about 350 megahertz (MHz) wide. This is the equivalent of all of the commercial AM, FM, and television broadcast channels plus shortwave, citizens' band, ham radio, and most public-service radio frequencies. Clearly, a cable system can carry a great deal of information!

Broadband cables can allocate the bandwidth available to three kinds of channels: (1) *dedicated channels* that are permanently assigned to pairs of communicating devices such as two computers, (2) *switched channels,* assigned to two devices on the request of a master controller, and (3) *shared channels* operating within their own network of devices using time-division techniques. Each group within these

Figure 4-16 This diagram illustrates the manner in which the frequencies on the WangNet broadband local network are allocated. This broadband system has so much capacity that significant portions of the spectrum are not even allocated. (Diagram courtesy of Wang Laboratories, Inc.)

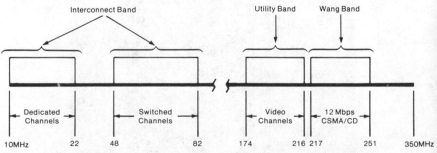

WangNet Frequency Allocations

allocations is unaware of the others. The common broadband cable appears to each to be a dedicated network medium. Broadband cables can mix many forms of information within a local network. Channels on the cable can be assigned to various data transmission functions, but video signals and voice transmissions can also be carried simultaneously.

The stations attached to a broadband cable use an RF modem to translate between the cable medium and their own internal electrical signaling system. If a station is required to operate only on one channel, it can have a reasonably simple fixed-frequency modem that listens and transmits on one limited frequency. If the station is to be

Figure 4-17 Fixed-frequency RF modems are used when the device needs to operate on only one channel assignment in the total spectrum of a broadband local network. (Diagram courtesy of Wang Laboratories, Inc.)

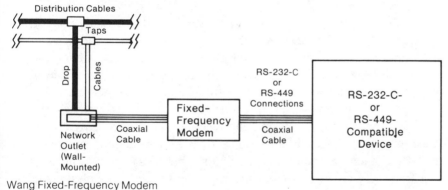

Figure 4-18 A frequency-agile RF modem is capable of moving to different channels in a broadband network and, in effect, operating in different subnetworks within the total network. (Diagram courtesy of Wang Laboratories, Inc.)

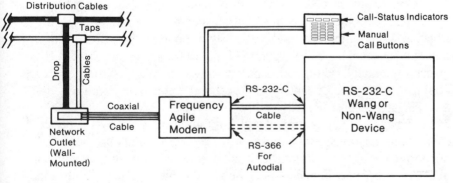

able to jump between networks (move to different channel frequencies), it can be equipped with a sophisticated multifrequency modem. These modems can be switched manually or by remote command of a cable controller (which probably is not the same device as a master network controller). These tunable modems are often referred to as *frequency-agile devices*. Obviously, increased sophistication can bring great information-transferring power, but also higher costs.

Broadband cables use two different kinds of physical configurations. The need for these configurations is caused by the simple fact that broadband cables are inherently unidirectional, like one-way streets or rivers. A station cannot send information directly to another station "upstream" from it. To overcome this limitation, there must be two one-way streets going in opposite directions. All information is transmitted on one street, goes down to the end of the cable, and returns on the other cable, where it can be received by all stations.

The two broadband configurations are *frequency translation* and the use of two *separate cables;* both arrangements separate the transmit and receive ports of an individual station. The first configuration, called *midsplit,* splits the available radio frequencies on the cable in half and dedicates one band of radio frequencies for station transmission and the other band of frequencies for station reception. The translation between transmission and reception is done by a *frequency converter.* This device is also referred to as a headend, frequency translator, or central retransmission facility, but it essentially functions as a frequency converter. The converter receives the transmissions of the network stations on what is termed the "return" channel, converts them to a different frequency, and rebroadcasts them on the "forward" channel.

The advantage of this midsplit system is that only one cable is used. This cuts the cost of installation and reconfiguration. On the negative side, since the midsplit system divides the cable into a transmit band and a receive band, the total usefulness of the cable is cut in half. (Actually, additional capacity is lost because of the need to establish a "no man's land" of guardband frequencies between the transmit and receive bands.)

The other kind of broadband configuration uses two separate cables, one for transmitting and one for receiving. This provides full use of the available bandwidth. One cable is used to transmit all signals to a passive connector, and another, separate cable is used to return the

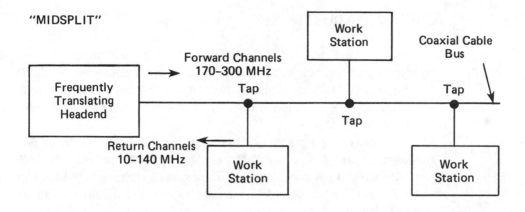

"MIDSPLIT"

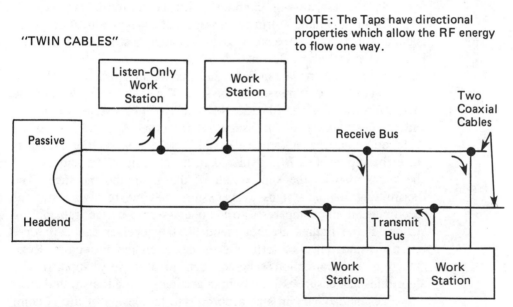

"TWIN CABLES"

NOTE: The Taps have directional properties which allow the RF energy to flow one way.

Figure 4-19 Broadband cables are designed in one of two different configurations, midsplit or twin. Each configuration has advantages and disadvantages in cost and capability.

signals that are still on the same frequency. This kind of system has a higher material cost to install, but it provides over twice as much capacity as a single-broadband cable arrangement. Its other technical advantages include the elimination of undesirable receiver and transmitter interaction at each station and the ability to connect listen-only subscribers (such as video displays) to the outbound cable.

61

MESSAGE ADDRESSING

So far, we have seen what kinds of media are used to connect the stations on a local network and how the time and frequencies available on the network are shared among the stations. We need to look briefly at how messages find their way between stations once they gain entry to the wire or cable.

There are three practical ways to route messages from the sender to the receiver: *message switching, packet switching,* and *time-division circuit switching.* A good example of message switching is the telex or telegram service. A complete message is developed, along with all information about the sender and recipient, and transmitted into the network. The transmission continues until the entire message is sent.

The most common form of message addressing on local networks is the use of packets. A packet of data is actually a string of characters. Each packet includes a destination address, a source address, and the message information. The message information in a packet may just be a fraction of the entire message to be sent. The packet may also include such information as an indication of what type of message it contains and a *checksum* of the message information. A checksum is an arithmetic number that can be derived in several ways. For example, since the digital data is considered to be a string of 0s and 1s, the checksum may be the sum of all of the 1s in the message. The transmitting station assigns a checksum, and the receiving stations recomputes it and compares it to the one assigned by the transmitting station. If the figures are not identical, the receiver can call for a retransmission. This is a form of error detection and correction. Error detection and correction schemes can involve very sophisticated algorithms that ensure extremely high accuracy in the transmitted data.

Packets can vary in size according to the design of the system. Some packets are of fixed length and others of variable length. Some systems may use packets 2000 characters long. Two thousand characters may sound like a large message instead of a compact packet, but it is small compared to the long streams of data transmitted by large computer systems. The size of the packet is determined by the designer, based on estimates of total message length, system speed, and other factors. Certain systems allow for variable-length packets. This improves system efficiency at the expense of more complex terminal software.

In packet switching, a block of data has addressing and possibly routing information added to it so that it can travel independently through relays and switches to its destination. Packets traveling independently through a system may even arrive out of order at the destination, but they can be rearranged by the network processor or the receiving station into the correct sequence to make a complete message.

A third alternative in digital switching is called time-division circuit switching. These systems use very small blocks of data (even just one character) as their transmission element. They avoid adding addressing and routing information to this small data block by the use of signaling channels that are separate from data channels. As the character or data block moves through the system, instructions go out on a separate line as to what to do with it. The coded instructions are simple, and the data channel is kept clear of all overhead. The throughput of the data channel can be very high. Time-division circuit switching is the newer technique and has not been developed as fully as packet switching.

IN REVIEW

This has been a long and meaty chapter, but the information clusters together easily into different methods of transmission, connection, traffic control, and addressing. Here are some things to remember:

Transmission Methods

- Media: wire, coaxial cable, fiber-optic cable.
- Coaxial cables provide good bandwidth and are the most common medium.
- Twisted-pair wire circuits can provide good economy under certain conditions.
- Fiber-optic systems provide tremendous bandwidth, but installation, maintenance, and expansion are potential problem areas unless you have experienced people available.

Connection

- Topology = geometry.
- The star network is commonly used with large central-computer systems.
- The ring network has advantages where all work is distributed, but it is vulnerable to disruption at any point.
- The bus or tree configuration is widely used and provides good flexibility and reliability.

Traffic Control

- Polling, reservation, and contention are schemes used to divide the available time among the stations on a system.
- Frequency-division multiplexing is a method of dividing the available space (frequency) among stations on a system.
- Broadband cables use frequency sharing to allow many stations to use the same cable at the same time.
- Both time- and frequency-division methods may be used on the same network or on the same medium.

Message Addressing

- Packets are blocks of information containing addressing information. They move around the system until they reach their destination. The information in the packets is then put together to make a complete message.
- Packet switching is most common, but systems that send complete messages are also used.
- Time-division circuit switching has potential for very high throughput.

Chapter 5

Technical Fundamentals and Standards

This chapter is optional reading. It deals with some of the fundamentals of electrical data transmission and with the standards and protocols that have been established. This kind of information normally is not the concern of a manager. The manager should only need to ask, "Can these devices exchange data? Do they need any special intermediate equipment to do so?"

This chapter will serve as a reference for questions you may have on technical matters. Readers involved in actual system design may find that a review of some of the electrical and protocol standards may lead to new insights into why certain practices became standard.

It is not necessary to understand the internal combustion engine in order to drive a car; similarly, it is not necessary to understand anything technical about data communications to use an electronic information-movement system. Knowing what is going on "under the hood," however, can ensure that you buy the equipment you need in the proper configuration, greatly increase the effectiveness of your system, and possibly reduce maintenance and repair bills.

STANDARDS AND PROTOCOLS

First, we have to introduce some more terms you should become familiar with. The first word is *standard*. A standard established by an international committee or industry organization can be very specific or very broad in nature. As an example, the Consultative Committee for International Telephone and Telegraph (CCITT) standard for the operation of a large packet-switching network is called X.25. It is a broad standard with many parts. It consists of three levels: the physical interface level, the frame level, and the network protocol level.

The *physical interface level* describes the physical and electrical interface between terminal equipment and devices like modems. The physical interface may be described by another standard called X.21.

The *frame level* describes the rules used for creating the block of information exchanged between the transmitting and receiving stations. This is a protocol or set of rules for message formulation and exchange. This interface is normally known as the *data link,* and this level may also be referred to as the *link level*. The international standard is called a High-Level Data-Link Control Procedure (HDLC). Many commercial companies have their own data-link control procedures.

The *network protocol level* describes how packets of information are formed and routed through a network. This protocol level can become very involved when it tries to anticipate all of the conditions that might exist on a network. It includes procedures for resetting the network, interrupting the authorized procedures, and many other functions.

Examples of three kinds of standards—electrical, message construction, and switching—will be discussed. The standards described here are commonly used, but they are only a few of the many that exist.

AN ELECTRICAL STANDARD: RS-232-C

Computers communicate internally and externally via digital signals. Inside every system, direct-current voltages are switched from moderate to very low many times a second. These changes in voltage represent digital bits of information. However, the voltages used differ from one system to another. Even in the microcomputer family, different microprocessors use different voltage levels. If all systems are to communicate on a common network, some standard for external voltage levels must be set. We need a solid definition of the electrical standards to be used. This has been supplied by the Electronic Industries Association (EIA) standard code RS-232-C. Outside the

United States this code is known as the International Consultive Committee Telephone and Telegraph (CCITT) code V.24. (It may also be considered a part of the CCITT standard X.21 which is recommended by the larger X.25 standard previously described. This code provides a common description of what the signal coming out of and going into the serial port of a computer or terminal will look like electrically. Specifically, RS-232-C provides for a signal swinging from a nominal + 12 volts to a nominal − 12 volts at certain specified current levels and resistive loads. The standard also defines the cables and connectors used to link data communications devices. Using this standard code simplifies the job of getting information in and out of a computer, terminal, or peripheral device. A new standard, called RS-449, which will eventually be a replacement or an alternative to RS-232-C, has been adopted, but compatibility with RS-232-C is specified in RS-449. (RS-449 has also been adopted as U.S. Federal Standard 1031.) The X.21 standard calls for a 15-pin connector; RS-232-C uses a 25-pin connector, and RS-449 calls for a 37-pin connector! As you can see, the establishment of a standard, even one as fundamental as an electrical standard, is not a simple task. However, RS-232-C will continue to be a useful signaling standard for many years to come, so let's see how it can be described.

The terms commonly used with electrical coding standards may be confusing. They are often carried over from other systems, but once you get them straight, they are easy to understand. Because of the peculiarities of solid-state logic devices, a *logic state* called "0" may not indicate 0 volts. Indeed, just the opposite is true. A logic state of 0 is defined as the positive voltage (+ 3 to + 24 volts) signal in RS-232-C. This is also known as a *space signal. Space* and *mark* are two designations held over from the days of mechanical printers, which are operated by electromagnets and driven by direct-current circuits. If you read any literature stating that a space should be transmitted, you know you are looking for a positive voltage or a 0 logic state.

The logic state of 1 is just the opposite. A logical 1 is a negative direct-current voltage; it is also known as a mark. You may wish to remember the sentence, "The teacher gave the student a low mark, but a logical one." The change in the direct-current voltage level serves as the signal or bit of information in the RS-232-C system. These bits are sensed, counted, and stored by data communications devices. The direct-current voltages used in this interconnection system can travel only about 50 feet before they lose their important electrical characteristics, so RS-232-C signaling is not used directly for long-distance communications. (The actual maximum effective DC path depends on many factors such as speed, cable type, and so on, but 50 feet is a standard for reliable high-speed service.) RS-232-C signaling is used to connect equipment divided into two groups: data terminal equipment (DTE) and data communications equipment (DCE). *Data terminal equipment* includes terminals of all kinds, computers, plotters, printers, and so on. *Data communications equipment* includes mainly modems and other special interconnection devices. RS-232-C is the most commonly used standard for local connection of computers, terminals, and modems.

RS-232-C is, however, just an electrical standard. It defines the voltage swings and other electrical parameters. It does not define what the voltage swings mean in terms of intelligent information. It is as if we said we will all use red and blue flags for signaling, but we had not defined what the position of the flags will mean. Another standard, a coding standard, is needed.

ASCII

The most commonly used coding standard is the American Standard Code for Information Exchange, or ASCII. ASCII is actually a data alphabet. Internationally, it is known as CCITT alphabet number 5. This alphabet not only tells us the coding of the electrical signals that make up the characters in ASCII, but it also provides useful numerical values for the characters and special standards for recording information on punch cards and magnetic media such as tape. ASCII defines the standard keyboard and provides codes for the smooth processing of information over data transmission systems.

ASCII defines certain coded signals as *control codes*. These are codes that usually mean something special to a machine. Control codes may tell electronic printers to tab, ring a bell, or begin a new page. They may stop the running of a computer program or turn on a tape drive. Control codes are valuable in data communications systems because of the flexibility they provide.

The coding of an ASCII character is easy to understand. The code essentially signifies how many times and when a voltage or tone goes high or low in a seven-bit sequence. The capital letter *A*, for instance, has a coding of 1000001. This would be coded over a piece of wire by sending one negative voltage (remember, a logic state of 1 is a negative voltage in RS-232-C signaling), five positive voltage pulses, and a final negative voltage pulse within certain time slots set by internal clocks in the equipment. Over a telephone line, the direct-current voltages would be converted to tones by a modem. The coding of the audio tones for the letter *A* would be one low tone, five high tones, and one low tone. This coding is also a number in the binary (base-2) number system. If the binary value is converted to the decimal (base-10) number system, it becomes 65. This coding of a mark, five space signals, and a mark always represents *A* and always has a decimal value of 65 in the ASCII alphabet. The number value of an ASCII character or a string of ASCII characters is often used in programs or transmission systems for sorting or checking data.

OTHER ALPHABET CODES

You may hear of other codes used for the transmission of alphabet characters. The simplest scheme, of course, is the *international Morse code*. In Morse, as it is commonly called, characters are represented by

Figure 5-1 The RS-232-C ASCII transmission of one character. The string of pulses represents one ASCII coded character transmitted using RS-232-C signaling. The width of the pulses changes directly with the baud rate. The actual voltages used may vary from +3 to +24 volts for a space to −3 to −24 volts for a mark.

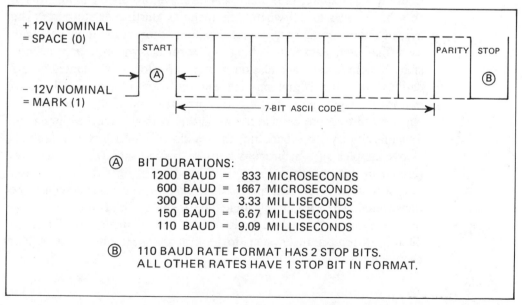

long and short pulses of light, sound, or electricity called dots and dashes. Morse code still finds some use in high-frequency radio transmission, but now it is often sent and received by electronic terminals equipped with microprocessors.

Baudot code is an older, standard automatic-printing-machine code which represents each character by five bits of data instead of ASCII's seven. It is often referred to as a five-level code. Machines using Baudot code are still common, and Baudot networks serving deaf users are operating in many parts of the country.

International Business Machines Corporation developed the "Extended Binary Coded Decimal Interchange Code," or EBCDIC. This eight-bit code is commonly used in connecting IBM equipment, particularly printing typewriters. Some software and hardware systems have been devised to allow communications between ASCII- and EBCDIC-speaking devices, but this is still not an easy task.

SYNCHRONOUS AND ASYNCHRONOUS TRANSMISSION

During the transmission of ASCII- or EBCDIC-coded characters, we need some way to tell when a character starts and stops. Two formats are used, one called *asynchronous* and the other called *synchronous*. Both formats require some additional information called *framing bits* to be sent in order to tell when a character is starting or stopping. The asynchronous format requires such framing information to be sent with each character. Packet switching is a form of synchronous transmission. Synchronous transmission gathers up blocks of characters and defines only the beginning and end of each block. Synchronous transmission is slightly faster and more efficient than asynchronous, but it requires more precise timing and is better suited to high-speed transmission systems handling thousands of characters per second. Two examples of synchronous format, bisync and HDLC, are described in this chapter.

The asynchronous format adds a *start bit* to each character to be transmitted. The start bit is a logical 0, or space, and is represented by the positive voltage level on the RS-232-C direct-current line. The start bit tells the receiving system to look at the next bits as an ASCII character.

At the end of the ASCII character, an eighth bit may be added for what is termed the *parity check*. This *parity bit* is a form of error detection and correction that can be used if the system designer wishes. The parity bit is given a value (1 or 0) to make the sum of the 1s in the eight-bit word come out to meet a predetermined standard—either odd or even. Standard practice is to make the parity odd in synchronous transmission and even in asynchronous. This serves as a constant check on the quality of the transmission. If the parity check is not the same as what the transmitter and receiver have been programmed to expect, various corrective actions could be taken. After the seven bits of ASCII character and the parity bit are sent, one or more *stop bits* (logic 1) are transmitted. These stop bits ensure that the receiver recognizes the next start bit, and the whole process starts over again, many times a second. The rate of transmission determines how many stop bits are transmitted. Two stop bits are usually used at 110 baud and below, and one during faster transmission.

DATA-LINK PROTOCOLS

ASCII and EBCDIC are two methods of coding characters into a data alphabet, but there are many other functions that must be performed before a block of information reaches its destination. These functions include addressing the data block, identifying the end of the message, and providing a check of message accuracy. These functions and many others are part of a complex set of network communications protocols that have been identified by various international committees and corporations.

Bisync

One of the most popular communications protocols is the bisync protocol developed by IBM. Like all synchronous communications protocols, *bisync* is simply a way of arranging the information to be transmitted and all the required overhead transmission data into a standard message format.

Bisync can be used for communications between many different kinds of digital equipment. It is referred to as a character-oriented protocol. Actions are taken according to the value of certain characters in the bisync message. This is in contrast to bit-oriented protocols, where shorter strings of bits perform network functions. Characters coded in the ASCII and EBCDIC alphabets can be transmitted using the bisync protocol. Bisync is a synchronous communications protocol. The receiving equipment synchronizes its timing circuits to match those of the transmitting system. Bisync can be used on networks with a master controller or those using contention schemes. It can be used in any network topology.

The main element of the bisync protocol is called a *message block*. It consists of a header, body, and trailer. The *header* is made up of two or more synchronization (sync or SYN) characters (source of the name *bisync*), a *start-of-header (SOH) character,* and addressing and control information for a particular receiving station.

The *trailer* contains the end-of-text character and the block-check character. Since the parity check of the ASCII character applies only for that character, the bisync protocol includes a method of checking the accuracy of the transmission of the entire block.

In actual practice, *padding* characters are added to the bisync block to ensure its reception. The beginning pad will usually be another sync character. The ending pad must be the number 1 in binary.

The identification of a station is easily done on a bisync network. Each station has a unique identification code from two to fifteen characters in length. This feature is needed in ring and bus networks, where every station on a bisync network transmits its own identification and the identification of the receiving station in every message block. This process takes network time, but it allows great flexibility.

Another kind of network protocol uses only bits instead of complete characters to perform network functions. This reduces the system time required to do various overhead functions. There are two of these link protocols you should know about: the High Level Data Link Control (HDLC) and Synchronous Data Link Control (SDLC).

HDLC and SDLC

High-Level Data-Link Control (HDLC) is an international standard developed by the International Standards Organization (ISO) in cooperation with several other European and North American organizations including the American National Standards Institute (ANSI). ANSI describes the standard as their X.366 Advanced Data Communication Control Procedure (ADCCP). HDLC is recommended in the frame level portion of the CCITT X.25 standard described at the beginning of this chapter. *Synchronous Data-Link Control (SDLC)* is a development of IBM. HDLC and SDLC are similar in structure and function. Indeed, protocols are used in equipment marketed by many different manufacturers. Sperry Univac has a Universal Data-Link Control and Burroughs has a Burroughs Data-Link Control, both based on HDLC. In theory, these protocols should allow equipment from different manufacturers to communicate together. In practice, the compatibility is almost never as complete as the theory would indicate. The following information is not specific to any of these protocols but is typical of them all. Anyone trying to design hardware or software to work with a specific manufacturer's protocol should obtain the latest technical information from that manufacturer.

In these bit-oriented protocols, the data message is sandwiched between a smaller number of characters than in bisync. The terminology changes slightly in that the message block used in bisync now becomes all or part of a group of bits called a *message frame*. Information about the address and other network overhead functions is contained in specific fields in the message frame.

The flag field is a unique combination of eight bits that is used to signal to receiving stations the beginning or end of a frame. It always has the binary code 01111110 (hex 7E).

The flag field is followed by an *address field*. The address field contains eight bits or some multiple of eight bits which identify the station to which the frame is addressed. A special address which is common to many or all stations may be used to lower the overhead time used in multiple addressing of messages.

The *control field* identifies the kind of transmission being made. A frame may be supervisory or may carry information. Various combinations of bits are used in the control field to signal what kind of frame is being sent. If an information frame is being transmitted, the first bit in the eight-bit control field will be set to a 0. The next three

Figure 5-2 This diagram illustrates the construction of one packet using IBM's SDLC bit-oriented format.

A PACKET IN THE IBM SYNCHRONOUS DATA LINK CONTROL (SDLC) FORMAT

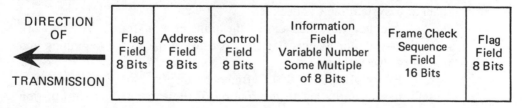

DIRECTION OF TRANSMISSION	Flag Field 8 Bits	Address Field 8 Bits	Control Field 8 Bits	Information Field Variable Number Some Multiple of 8 Bits	Frame Check Sequence Field 16 Bits	Flag Field 8 Bits

bits are the sequence number of the frame relative to previous information frames transmitted by the same station. This sequence number is used to identify packets and to call for retransmissions or to perform corrections.

The control field performs several important identification functions. If the 'control field is to signal that a supervisory command is being transmitted, the first bit of the field will be set to 1. The second bit will be set to 0. The third and fourth bits are used to signal that a previous frame was accepted or rejected or should be retransmitted or that a station is busy.

The control field may also be used to signal link and network control functions. This use of the frame is signaled by setting both the first and second bits in the control field to 1. The remaining bits represent certain network messages having to do with response modes, disconnection, and system operation.

The *information field* follows the control field. It can be any number of bits, but usually some multiple of eight. The maximum length of the information field is set by the system designer based on factors such as the number of stations on a network and the nature of the messages or data to be transmitted. The only real limiting factor is the size of the receiving storage buffer in the equipment on the system.

The *frame-check-sequence field* provides a numerical check on the message for the purpose of error detection and correction. The frame-check sequence normally uses a common error-checking routine called *cyclic redundancy check 16 (CRC16)*. The transmitting station calculates a number which is the binary result of the entry of the value of the address, control, and information fields (value X) into the formula $X^{16} + X^{12} + X^5 + 1$. The receiving station makes the same calculation and compares the two numbers. If they are identical, the frame is assumed to be correct. If they are not the same, the receiving station issues a rejection notice (in the form of a supervisory frame) and requests a retransmission. This transmission-check-retransmission sequence can be repeated a number of times. System designers usually put a limit on the number of retransmissions (seven to ten) permitted until a system fault is declared.

Another flag field closes the transmission frame. All network stations monitor for this flag field because it marks the beginning and end of every frame.

Every HDLC or SDLC frame or bisync block contains some information important to the routing of these packets of information through a communications network. They are an overlapping part of the next protocol layer described by the X.25 standard, the packet-level layer.

NETWORK PROTOCOLS

The division between the network level and the frame level of a protocol is more difficult to define than the difference between the frame level and the physical and electrical standard. The difference is often purely one of a functional concept rather than of physical or electrical configuration. But that concept is quite important to understanding the entire architecture of an information-movement system.

The network layer in a packet network provides a set of rules and standard procedures used by equipment on a network to establish connection to the network, move packets of information through the network, detect and correct errors, and perform other network functions.

It is the packet-network-level software that actually examines the address of the data packet and properly addresses replies. This level performs the error check and requests retransmission as appropriate. This level of software also establishes what is termed a logical channel with another communications device. In a packet-switched network, a *logical channel* is the path a packet takes on its trip between equipment and the exchange of information needed to get it there. In a circuit-switched system, the network-level software directs the establishment of a logical channel which is also an electrical transmission circuit.

THE TOTAL NETWORK

The technical standards and network protocols described in this chapter work together to move information between processing and display devices. They make up a large portion of the technical function of a local network, but they should be invisible to the practical functions of the network. The users of a network should never have to think or worry about the electrical or network standards in use. Unfortunately, some low-level electrical or signaling standards (such as the difference between ASCII and EBCDIC) can make a great difference in the ability of the network to transfer information. The next chapter will give a perspective on the total network and the relationship of the parts of the network. But first, here are some things to remember about technical standards and protocols:

- CCITT X.25 is an important standard describing how computers, terminals, and communications devices such as modems hook together and operate on a network.

    It has many substandards that specify various physical, link, and network connections.

- Signaling standards, such as RS-232-C, specify what kinds of voltages and connectors will be used to link equipment.

- Coding standards or data alphabets, such as ASCII, Baudot, or EBCDIC, give meaning to the electrical information provided by the signaling standard.

- Synchronous and asynchronous transmission methods are different ways of grouping characters for transmission. Asynchronous is commonly used in local connections between computer and terminal equipment. Synchronous transmission is used more commonly in high-speed computer-to-computer circuits. Bisync is a form of synchronous transmission commonly used in IBM equipment.

- An interrelated series of control protocols deals with the movement of information between stations on a communications link or line. These data-link-control protocols have many names. The most common are IBM's Synchronous Data-Link Control and the International Standards Organization's High-Level Data-Link Control.

    The protocols divide a block of data into various sections called fields. These data fields provide the block type, address, and information along with an error-detection- and -correction function.

- Network protocols determine how messages are routed around a network and control the functions of the network, such as marking stations in or out of service, and so on.

Chapter 6

A Standard Network

OSI (OPEN SYSTEM INTERCONNECTION)

SNA (SYSTEMS NETWORK ARCHITECTURE)

The number of companies and businesses manufacturing data processing equipment with a data communications capability is growing quickly. Some of these devices are only pieces of a total network. They need some common conceptual basis to be integrated into the network plan or architecture. The elements of data communications described in chapter 5—signaling, coding, and network transmission—are working standards. They have been in daily use for many years. But, because of differences in design and actual application, computer and terminal systems produced by different manufacturers still probably will not operate together on a network without extensive custom designing.

This chapter will introduce two models of a communications network. The first is an international model established for many kinds of systems. The second is a model established by IBM.

THE OSI MODEL

The problems of compatibility between the systems of different manufacturers were recognized early, but little was done to find a solution until 1977. In that year, the International Standards Organization (ISO) chartered a committee (Special Subcommittee 16 of Techni-

OPEN SYSTEMS INTERCONNECTION MODEL

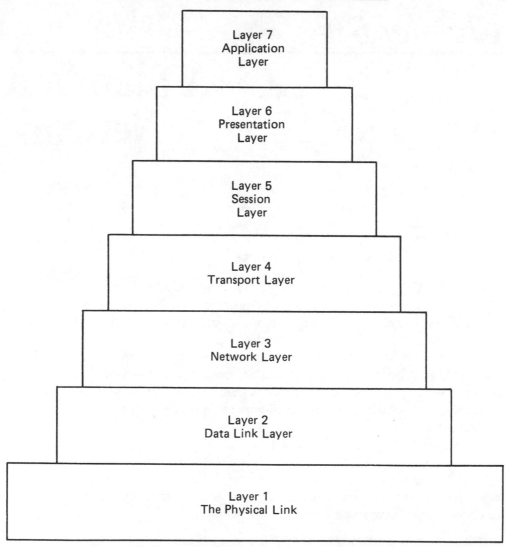

Figure 6-1 The Open System Interconnection model is designed to define the functional jobs that must be done when transferring information. Some layers become more important in certain kinds of networks than others. Several functional layers may actually be combined in one physical piece of equipment or one communications program.

cal Committee 97) to study the problem of compatibility in data network equipment. Their work continued for a number of years and led to the publication of several versions of the Open System

Interconnection (OSI) Reference Model. The term *open system* essentially means a system open to equipment from different manufacturers. This OSI reference model is useful for anyone involved in purchasing or managing a local network because it provides a theoretical framework on which you can hang practical opportunities and problems.

The design of such an open system has proven to be a very difficult task because of (1) all the manufacturers and standards organizations involved and (2) the size of the problem. It involves much more than just electrical signaling.

A local network must be thought of as a single entity. The system has many parts, but they all interrelate. The OSI model provides names for the parts of a communications network. It doesn't matter in a general sense if the network is local or international. The size of the network may limit or increase the importance of certain of its parts, but they will all be there in one form or another. The OSI model uses specific definitions to describe the various portions of the network. It speaks of "layers" of functions arranged in a hierarchy. This gives the impression that they are all neatly stacked, with firm boundaries between them. This is not the way they operate in the real world. In a real system, one printed-circuit board might perform almost all of the functions called for in several layers of the model. Still, the model provides a good way to structure your understanding of a network. It also acquaints you with more of the concepts and jargon used by professionals in the industry. Throughout this description we will use the term *layer* because the industry uses it. Please think of each layer as a *function* that must be performed.

The Application Layer

The OSI model has seven functional layers. The top function, the one you should always keep in mind, is the end-user application. This is where the machines talk to the people. If this application isn't properly handled, the entire system is useless. The goal of any communications system is to serve the user when and how the user wants to be served. It is interesting to note how often this is turned on its head and we find the user serving the system. The ISO committee calls this layer 7 in their model.

The *application layer* is concerned with the information in the message and how well it serves the user. There are no firm protocols or standards for this function except those of common sense, utility, and logic. There are many common practices, but they are tied to the functional program being used and cannot be discussed here. The application layer is the most critical layer, but your common sense defines it.

The Presentation Layer

The next down in the model (layer 6) is the presentation function. The *presentation layer* prepares the information for the application. An example of this function is the conversion of a file received from a brand-X word processor into the proper format for display on a brand-Y system. Each word processor might use different codes to set the ends of paragraphs or the length of a page. The presentation function would have to know the differences and provide for them. This could be done in hardware, but it is more likely to be done in software.

Figure 6-2 This is a photograph of the Xerox 8010 Star information system. The Star has strong communications capabilities, but in terms of the OSI model, particular attention has been given to the presentation and application layers. Special software displays functions such as document filing and creation in graphic form. The need for computer knowledge and keyboard (typing) skills is greatly reduced. The device in the man's right hand is called a "mouse." It rolls over the desk and controls the position of the cursor on the screen. This easy-to-use feature eliminates the need to find arrows or other commands to move work around on the screen. (Photo courtesy of the Xerox Corporation. All rights reserved.)

Figure 6-3 This closer view of the screen of the Xerox 8010 Star information system shows the variety of typefaces and sizes as well as graphics abilities that are available. Most Star functions are available by simply moving a pointer and pressing a key. (Photo courtesy of the Xerox Corporation. All rights reserved.)

The Session Layer

The *session layer* (layers 5) is a coordinating function. It establishes the communications link between units (like between the two word processors above) and gradually feeds or buffers the information to the devices or program performing the presentation function. The session layer also provides the sometimes critical identification and authentication functions. It recognizes users and acknowledges both their arrival and departure. In some systems, the session layer can be a driving factor in system design. In others, it is a very small consideration. When it is most important, this job might be done by a separate micro- or minicomputer. In its minimum form, this job could be done by a couple of small integrated circuits.

The Transport Layer

The *transport layer* (layer 4) functions to provide a common face to the communications network. It translates whatever unique requirements

Figure 6-4, Figure 6-5 Digital Microsystems provides a terminal as a part of their HiNet local-network system, which also has unique presentation capabilities. The screen on the System 5000 can be changed to either a vertical or a horizontal display for different types of work. In the vertical orientation, the system can function as a full-page word processor displaying 80 characters by 66 lines. In the horizontal orientation, the system can provide a traditional-size screen of 80 columns by 26 lines of very high resolution characters or an extrawide screen of 132 characters by 50 lines. (Photos courtesy of Digital Microsystems.)

the other higher layers might have into something the network can understand. It also makes the most effective use of whatever various communications media it is connected to and selects the best or most logical route for transmission. It detects and corrects errors in transmission and provides for the expedited delivery of priority messages. It checks the data, puts it into the proper order if it came in wrong, and usually sends an acknowledgment back to the originating transport layer. It attempts to reestablish contact in the event of a network failure.

Several industry and governmental standards exist for a transport function in data communications devices. The U.S. Department of Defense has adopted a transmission-control protocol (TCP) that has many functions and options. The Bell System has also released a protocol called BX.25 which describes, among other things, the transport, session, and presentation functions.

The transport function is an important part of any communications device. It would normally involve both hardware and software and be specially configured to match both the equipment it is on and the network it serves.

The Network Layer

The *network layer* (layer 3) sets up a logical transmission path through a switched network. In local networks this path may only be theoretical, since the individual units are almost always electrically connected into the circuit and the paths are defined by the network topology. But in large systems, several transmission paths and even alternative media (dialed telephone service versus leased service, for example) may exist. The transmission path may be temporary in nature—lasting only long enough to transfer a packet of information—or it may provide continuous connection for two users of the network.

In a local network, the network control function can exist in one place (star network) or be distributed (bus or ring.) It is essentially made up of software that recognizes various conditions on the network and reacts to them.

The Data-Link Layer

The *data-link layer* (layer 2) does the accounting and traffic-control chores needed to transfer information on an electrical link. It forms the information to be moved into strings of characters such as those used in IBM's bisync communications protocol or into blocks of bits such as those used by the HDLC protocol described in chapter 5. The data-link layer functions like the foreman in a railroad yard who is making up a train. It puts every piece of information into the right place and checks it out before putting it on the tracks. Similarly, incoming information is broken down and properly routed within the receiving device.

The data link was originally thought of as being a function of the software in a device. It is increasingly being done by special-purpose integrated circuits requiring little external programming.

The Physical Layer

This functional level can be very troublesome and occupy the time of an expensive technician if it is not properly planned. The *physical layer* (layer 1) describes the electrical and physical connection between communicating units. It is often the most visible and sometimes a very troublesome part of the system, but it shouldn't be.

In 1960 the Electronic Industries Association (EIA) established an electrical standard for interconnection called RS-232. The standard has been revised three times, and the most current standard is called RS-232-C. RS-232-C is an electrical signaling standard. It conforms closely to the international X.27, X.26, V.11, and V.10 standards. This means that equipment (such as a modem and a terminal) that conforms to these standards should be able to work together on the most basic electrical level.

There are other electrical standards, such as IEEE-488, that are also commonly used for the interconnection of certain kinds of communicating equipment. Equipment designed under this standard will not operate with RS-232-C equipment.

RS-232-C will gradually be replaced by a newer standard, RS-449. However, RS-449 equipment should be electrically compatible with RS-232-C equipment (although the cables are not the same).

X.25

The three lowest layers of the OSI standard—the network, data-link, and physical interfaces—are described by a number of existing standards. The most commonly referenced standard is Recommendation X.25 of the Consultative Committee for International Telephone and Telegraph (CCITT). Recommendation X.25 was adopted in 1976. It has been modified many times and has several variations.

Not all manufacturers support all portions of X.25, but it is becoming increasingly important as a standard. It is the best thing we have to describe the connection between equipment on a public packet-switching network. The recommendations of X.25 carry over into local networks with little or no change. The technical specifications of X.25 and other standards and recommendations have been provided for reference in chapter 5.

IBM AND SNA

IBM began promoting its Systems Network Architecture (SNA) in 1975. SNA is a network architecture or plan like the OSI architecture. Like the OSI architecture, it describes the various jobs to be done by stations communicating in a network in terms of a series of functions or levels. The OSI architecture and SNA have many similarities, but the names differ. SNA's levels are described differently from those in the OSI architecture. The description of SNA includes many specific terms, such as *node, network-addressable unit, physical unit,* and *logical unit.*

An *SNA node* is a general term for a central processing unit (computer), a communications controller, and the local communications elements. SNA can be applied to any size network covering any geographical area, so it also defines the methods of communications between nodes. SNA defines subarea nodes and peripheral nodes. Essentially, *subarea nodes* can communicate between themselves while *peripheral nodes* can only communicate with a subarea node.

Network-addressable units are the hardware and software within terminals and computers that interface with the network. This is not a difficult idea to express conceptually, but in a terminal or computer the network-addressable unit may consist of several pieces of hardware and software that can serve several different functions. There are two kinds of network-addressable units, the *logical unit* and the *physical unit.* The terms simply indicate the difference between the software the user sees (logical unit) and the equipment the network sees (the physical unit.)

The top level of the SNA structure is the end-user services layer. The end user may be a person, a device, or even an operating program. In their later literature, IBM calls this the *services-manager layer.*

The second layer of SNA is called *presentation services.* This layer provides the interface between the end user and the network. It gives the using person or device certain rules, capabilities, and methods of using the network.

The third layer, the *data-flow–control services,* determines if units on the network will operate in the half-duplex or full-duplex mode. It will "chain" together messages or parts of messages that can be logically grouped because they are going to the same receiving station. It also groups data according to specific transactions (the airline reservation for a certain customer, for example), if that is appropriate.

The next layer, the *transmission-control layer,* provides the protocol used between two communicating devices to control and acknowledge the transfer of information. The transmission-control layer constructs the message headers and attaches them to the message. The headers are useful in performing the session-level pacing function.

This function simply means that communicating units pace their transmission speeds based on acknowledgments and message numbers contained in the message headers.

The *path-control layer* provides the logic to route messages through a network. The path-control logic determines how a message travels when more than one route exists in a multiconnection network.

The *data-link–control layer* performs the important function of error detection and correction. It detects errors occurring during transmission and requests retransmission. Data-link control may use the SDLC protocol or a protocol called *channel data-link control,* common in IBM 370-series mainframe computer systems.

These SNA functions combine to create, route, control, transmit, and acknowledge messages flowing through a network. This description of SNA has been condensed to the point where an IBM designer would barely recognize it, but it serves to give you a feeling for the kind of structure involved in SNA and the functions that are addressed.

SNA is not commonly used as a local network standard, but local networks may have to connect to SNA systems through protocol translators, which are computers themselves.

A SYSTEM PERSPECTIVE

The purpose of this chapter has been to give you a theoretical perspective on what goes on inside a data communications system. Moving information is complex work, and there are many jobs to be done. It is important never to be so overcome by the technical details that you forget the goal of an information-movement and processing system: service to the user.

THINGS TO REMEMBER

- A total information-movement system can be described in terms of the jobs to be done. These jobs range from electrical connection to manipulation of the data by the user.
- There is a bewildering array of technical standards and recommendations describing how most of the jobs should be done. The presence of all of these standards does not guarantee that communicating equipment will operate together on a data network.
- The IBM System Network Architecture describes the functions to be performed while moving information through a communications network. It is not a specific local network architecture, but it may be a part of a network, or a local network may have to interact with an SNA system.

Chapter 7

Managing
the Data Base

What is the data base and where is it? Those simple-sounding questions can drive a great many decisions and actions when you have to decide how to move the information in that data base around between various users.

FINDING THE INFORMATION

One of your first jobs is to figure out where the information is right now. If your business is like most, a great deal of the information needed to do business is still on paper. The transition from paper to electronic data will not take place overnight or even over a period of months. In most cases, it will not be possible to load all or even a major portion of the information presently on paper into the electronic system. The transition from paper to electronic systems will occur in very small but steady steps taken on a daily basis. That's OK—we have to start sometime. Regardless of what form the information your business uses is in—paper, electronic, or all in one person's head—you have to determine who develops most of the information and who needs to see it.

A lot of these information estimates can be initially made by a single corporate executive or planner, but it is probably wise to take advantage of this opportunity to involve the potential users of an information-movement system at a relatively early stage. There are several ways to gain a picture of where the information is and where it needs to go. The most common methods are survey, interview, and observation.

An Information Survey

One way to identify your potential data base is through a *survey* form. One caution is in order here: KISS—that is, Keep It Super Simple! Don't use any technical jargon and do help your subjects by providing a menu of choices. Don't ask them for original thinking yet. At this point, probably only the executives are thinking creatively; everyone else is going around wondering what this will mean to his or her job.

A good place to start with a survey of this kind is at the photocopy machine. If information is being copied, it obviously has some importance and more than one destination. This kind of information should be identified and captured electronically. (Don't, however, use your copier survey as an excuse for a crackdown on all the "unofficial" copying being done. You will sabotage your project from the beginning. Discrete use of the copy machine for personal papers has come to be an expected "perk" for modern office workers. Tilt at this windmill if you like, but don't use your information survey as a shield.)

You can post survey forms (actually a detailed activity log) at places like the copy machine where information is processed or handled. You should also circulate survey forms to individuals working in activities that create, distribute, or move information.

Figure 7-1 Sample survey form.

Copier Log Sheet

We are trying to determine how information moves around in our business. Please fill out this log whenever you use the copier. This survey will continue for one month. Thank you.

Description of the Original Document:	Your Office:	Copies Going To:

You may have to develop several survey forms that are more specific to certain departments and even to certain jobs within the department. This is a good way to find out what is happening in the business and great training for a junior executive.

Interviews

Many people cause information to move in an organization. They may be very senior or very junior in the structure, but for some reason information flows to or through them. Such people are bookkeepers, personnel managers, purchasing agents, freight and shipping clerks, financial managers, and operational administrators. Because of their importance and the need to win their support, these people should be personally contacted and asked about their use and manipulation of information. It isn't enough to ask them to fill out a survey; they need the personal touch.

The purpose of such an interview should be stated at the very start. It should be described as only informal research and tentative in nature. The interview questions don't have to be detailed, but they may require that the people you are interviewing do a little research. If such details as the approximate number of forms being processed or the destination of certain information are not immediately available, you should come back after the people have had some reasonable time for research.

The Interview Process

These interviews should be conducted in the person's work area. In this setting the individual is surrounded by familiar objects that will serve as reminders and examples of the immediate information flow. The time of day and time in the business cycle should be selected so that the person being interviewed doesn't feel pressured by higher priorities (such as going home!). First, explain the purpose of the study in the most simple, nontechnical, and nonthreatening terms possible. Here is an example:

INTERVIEW TEXT

I want to talk to you for a few minutes about how you get the information you need to do your job. By information, I mean forms, notes, letters, pieces of paper, and phone calls. I just want to make a little list (maybe a sketch) of how information comes to you and where it goes when it leaves you. I'm doing this with a lot of people because we are trying to understand how information flows and how we can make it flow better.

From whom do you get outside mail or packages?

To whom do you send outside mail?

From whom do you get internal company mail?

To whom do you send company mail?

Do you receive any charts or graphs?

Do you create any charts or graphs?

Do you get any other informal notes or written communications?

Can you estimate how many phone calls you get in a day?

Are the majority from within the company or outside?

What departments (persons) call you from within the company?

Whom do you call?

Do you have a busy time of the week, month, or season when you have to send and receive more information than usual?

Observation

There are a lot of other clues as to where the important information resides. Most of these clues can be found through observation. Look at the labels on the frequently used eye-level drawers of filing cabinets. Look at what is contained in the filing cabinets nearest to a working area. Examine the interoffice mail envelopes and see who is sending mail and where it is going. Inspect the operating reports and try to diagram where the information that goes into each report came from.

Go through the offices after hours and look at desk tops. What do people have on their desks, tacked up on their office walls, or within easy reach? Some studies have shown that one of the most important unorganized corporate assets is a list of relevant names and telephone numbers. How many telephone lists do you see? How much time do other people spend looking for the same numbers?

Once you become sensitive to the flow of information within a business, you will know a lot more about the business and have an initial image of what kind of electronic system will make that information readily available.

A CENTRALIZED
OR DISTRIBUTED SYSTEM?

The first characteristic of an electronic system that your information survey should point toward is whether the processing power and memory of the system should be distributed, centralized, or a hybrid of both. The introduction of relatively inexpensive processing power into desk-top computers has made the line between distributed and centralized systems very difficult to find. Still, certain central data bases will probably stand out.

An existing accounting computer may well become the hub of an information-movement system because of the monies already invested in hardware, software, and the development of procedures. This data base may be critical to the usefulness of a planned executive-information system. If you have some critical information on a computer system, such as accounting data, determine who else would benefit from access to that information and who else could improve the quality of information by making inputs. Your challenge is how to get the needed information in and out of the accounting computer without hindering the accounting function. If we can use a few of the terms from chapter 6, the OSI standard would say you have to improve the transport and session layers of the existing system while not harming the application layer.

Any other existing electronic data base, even the disk files of a word processor, should be included in your information diagram. Don't overlook Telex machines and computer terminals that may be hidden away in engineering offices. These existing files are a large asset that should be factored in when decisions about system design are being made.

STRUCTURE AND STRIFE

After you have charted where the information is, draw a few lines showing where it comes from and where it goes and look for trends. These lines will show you how an electronic system would have to gather, hold, and move data. They will also show you some of the realities of your physical and economic situation. Organizational structures are developed and maintained for many reasons. Sometimes organizations are structured along lines of personality or tradition. One of the most rational reasons for using a particular organizational structure is that it improves corporate communications. If the corporate structure limits business communications, then don't automate a bad structure. It will not function any better; things will just work badly faster.

Here is another practical warning: A computerized bad practice is still a bad practice. It was stressed in an earlier chapter that an information-movement system should not direct how functions are done. But similarly, we should not waste computer power on problems that computerization won't solve.

Don't store trivia. Not all information needs to be in the data base. A good example is shown by the initial advertising for the home computer. You probably saw ads promising that home computers would be a miracle in the kitchen because each cook would be able to store a complete file of recipes in the computer and have them ready whenever needed. The truth is, it simply is not practical to store kitchen recipes on a home computer. They are more difficult to retrieve and the computer usually comes out covered with flour. There is no substitute for a recipe file box for keeping information that is infrequently accessed by only one or two persons.

In a modern business, certain records are infrequently accessed and have no real bearing on any other information or reports. These items should stay on file cards or in ledger books. Look for the kind of information that is frequently accessed by many people (or a few key people) and that is involved in other files or reports.

SOME CASE STUDIES

The case-study method is often useful for illustrating how certain conditions might be met. Here are three case studies that illustrate three different kinds of problems and possible solutions.

Manufacturing Firm

This company is involved in light metal fabrication. When they started to consider the need to improve their information-management system they had one IBM computer for accounting and another for inventory control. They had five Xerox word processors spread among three locations in different parts of the building.

The office copier log provided the most valuable information on the information flow in this company. It showed that the secretaries spent a great deal of time copying outgoing correspondence for each other's files and that the accounting department copied large weekly operating reports for several senior managers. Other functions, such as purchasing and personnel, copied handwritten reports that were carried to accounting for entry into the management report data base.

Consultants recommended that this company initially needed two separate networks. The first network would link the word processors to provide an expanded data base for correspondence and electronic mail. Existing telex equipment would be included in the correspondence network. The second network would link the IBM machines and add executive work stations in the corporate offices. It would also provide improved computer support for the purchasing department. It was recommended that as the existing computer equipment was depreciated from the corporate books, additional steps be taken to provide an interface between the correspondence network and an expanded accounting–inventory-control network.

Engineering Consulting Firm

This mechanical engineering consulting firm had several terminals with printers and plotters that were used for access to a time-sharing service. The ten staff engineers shared one minicomputer, and several had brought in their own desk-top computers. All typing was done by three secretaries on electric typewriters.

The data communications consultants found personal interviews provided the most valuable information in this organization. The younger engineers had good ideas about the flow of information, and the more senior members of the firm supported them. The consultants recommended a system made up of desk-top microcomputers sharing a large central memory. The central memory contained many programs and data files that could be accessed by the distributed microcomputers. The secretarial work stations accessed the same data base. The microcomputers functioned as terminals when it was necessary to use the time-sharing service. One terminal and plotter were retained because of their unique graphic capabilities. The minicomputer was eliminated and the majority of its useful programs made available to the distributed network.

This arrangement decreased the use of the expensive time-sharing service, increased the power available to each individual engineer, and eliminated the minicomputer. It significantly reduced the time needed to prepare engineering reports because columns of figures were produced automatically by data-base management programs without tedious typing.

It is significant to note that the company became very vulnerable to the failure of the single shared hard-disk memory. The consultants recommended that critical files be transferred to other storage media (floppy disk) on at least a daily basis. They also recommended the purchase of a second shared disk for backup as soon as possible.

Government Office

Over 140 employees in this government office spent their productive time almost evenly between working with paper, using the telephone, and sitting in meetings. Questionnaires provided good insight into how the data flowed in this organization. The lines of data flow were complex. They went up and converged with the chief administrator, as would be expected, but there was also a large crossflow of information within the agency and between this and other agencies. Twelve word processors were augmented by numerous typewriters. Amazingly, this agency had nearly 2.8 four-drawer filing cabinets per employee.

The task of capturing the huge amount of information already on paper staggered the consultants who looked into this government agency. They concentrated on building a future data base and eliminating inefficient information transfer methods. A survey of telephone calls found that about 17 percent of the outgoing calls and only 10 percent of incoming calls were successfully completed on the first attempt. The consultants recommended the installation of a sophisticated computerized branch telephone exchange with call-forwarding, automatic re-dialing, and call-waiting functions. The same exchange was used to route documents between the existing word processors over dedicated circuits. It was recommended that a minicomputer be installed in the administrative office of the chief executive to serve as an electronic mail system and a central communications point. Reasonably inexpensive terminals would be installed in offices at the rate of one per three or four professional workers to be used for document preparation, research, and filing. Because of the ingrained and established procedures for dealing with information on paper, moderately priced dot-matrix printers were included with the terminals.

The results of this study were not clear because the recommendations were put into practice over an extended period of time. It appears that the branch exchange initially made some improvement in the number of incoming calls successfully completed the first time. The electronic mail system was little used at first, but interest from a new chief executive caused an increased use of the system, which resulted in fewer hours spent per week in meetings.

NO "SILVER BULLET"

Distributed-information networks are those that have the information available throughout the system. Centralized information systems keep all of the data bank in one place. These case studies illustrate that there is no single best way to store or move information around in a business or organization. A total, integrated network may be an end goal, but the capital outlay may be high and the payback difficult to quantify.

Salespeople representing firms with modular and distributed systems will assure you that the modular approach is best. It allows for growth and flexibility. Representatives from companies with centralized products will point out the benefits of simplicity, centralized control, and a shared data base. The practical solution will probably be a combination of techniques, so the theoretical titles lose a lot of their meaning. Most modern systems do some degree of information sharing and local terminal processing. But the best way to determine what your information-movement system will look like is to find out where the data are and where they need to go.

DATA SECURITY

Corporate papers locked in a safe are secure. When the information contained on those papers is introduced into an electronic system, the physical security of the information may be compromised in different ways. Notice that the meaningful word in the last sentence is *physical*. Although we hear about many crimes in which persons steal or alter data from computers, there is invariably a physical insecurity that leads to the electronic crime. Investigation of corporate theft from computer systems shows that it would often have been easier for a thief to steal information on paper than information in a computer.

The password and protection schemes on data movement and processing systems can be excellent. There is always some physical link, however, that can provide an access key. It is impossible to overestimate the cleverness of a thief looking for information. Unfortunately, many people do. Passwords and access codes are often written in places where innocent people think they will appear meaningless. Favorite spots are on desk and wall calendars, on desk blotters or under the glass on the desks, even on the wall next to the terminal. These innocent deviations from procedure are open invitations to information thieves, embezzlers, and industrial saboteurs.

Some of the physical precautions needed to protect corporate data would be obvious if the data was on paper, but they become more complex when the data is in digital form.

Physical Access

Most companies have found it wise to control at least the physical access to the corporate area. This can be done in effective ways that are less threatening and expensive than using locked gates. Corporate reception areas are common in business. Similarly, some physical barrier around critical information-processing equipment can significantly restrict the opportunities for unauthorized persons to learn things they do not need to know.

Strong control over the physical access to equipment and terminals is the best way to prevent unauthorized access to or manipulation of data files. The tapes and disks that hold corporate data should be given appropriate protection. They should be duplicated regularly and the backup disks stored in a separate place.

Data Access

Modern information-storage or -movement systems are equipped with excellent password and authorization-code schemes. These schemes can theoretically be broken by expert teams with unlimited resources, but if such people are your enemies, you need help anyway! Password systems are perfectly acceptable for protecting corporate and institutional data, as long as a few rules are followed:

- Make the password or access code truly random. Birthdates and initials, the names of offspring and spouses, Social Security numbers, and street addresses are examples of very poor password codes. This kind of information can be easily gathered by someone motivated to gain access to a system.
- Keep the codes long. Many passwords can be over twenty characters long. Users should be encouraged to use a nonsense sentence, including spaces, numbers, letters, and even control codes to make the job of a code breaker much more difficult.
- Keep the codes absolutely private.

- Keep the codes memorized.
- Keep only one master list in a very safe place.
- Change codes frequently and immediately when an employee leaves.

Audit

Auditing computer systems has become an art in itself. One important tool of auditors (and programmers, managers, and accountants, too) is an audit-trail diagram. This diagram traces the steps a business or administrative transaction goes through. It shows, in block-diagram form, who initiates an action, who performs activities related to the action, who approves the results at certain points, and what the end result should look like. This kind of diagram is a powerful training and management tool. It takes some time to build, but the initial investment will be paid back many times over by eliminating the need to research the process and "reinvent the wheel" several times a year.

The audit record-keeping function should include a description of the critical data that are needed to reconstruct files in the event of disaster or sabotage.

Internal auditors (managers and supervisors) should receive automatically generated reports on inventory and cash discrepancies, large movements of funds, or large inventory reductions.

Managers and supervisors should be alert to differences in the way a system or program functions when certain individuals are on vacation or have left the job. If a function seems to run faster or consistently give results even a few pennies higher, a long-term "tap" could have been operating.

Customer mailing lists have become valuable commodities. A wise manager might put a "dummy" address in the mailing list; mail sent to this name and address would signal that the list was being used.

The key to the electrical security of electronic systems and data is the physical security of the systems and the procedures used to access information. Proper physical-security procedures and appropriate audits can eliminate the most common threats.

LONG-RANGE PLANNING

The surveys, interviews, and observations you make will give you a picture of the current information-management situation in your organization. The equipment and systems you invest in this year, however, are likely to be with you for a minimum of five years (under present tax-depreciation schedules). It would be wise to have some idea of where the company is going and what its needs will be in the future.

It is a fact of life that most businesses do not have a very extensive long-range plan. Industrial management consultants are usually happy to find two-year plans in any but the most far-sighted firms. It would be very helpful if the management of your company or organization would provide some statement—however brief—of objectives for the next two to five years and some description of what strategies will be used to meet these objectives. The strategies can be analyzed for their impact on the corporate structure and on the processing and movement of information in the organization.

Long-range plans are certainly little more than educated guesses, but they serve to give some legitimacy and purpose to your description of the data-base storage, manipulation, and movement requirements of your organization.

THINGS TO REMEMBER

Here are some things to remember about the data base of information you will want to process and move:

- It is important to find out where the information is now so you know how and where it moves.
- Many different techniques can be used to find the data base:
  Survey forms
  Interviews
  Observation
- Some data are too difficult or simply not worth capturing in an electronic data base.
- It is likely that some existing electronic data bases must be considered.
- Computerizing a bad practice does not make it work better.
- The phrases *distributed data base* and *centralized data base* are becoming more theoretical than real. Most modern systems do some degree of data sharing and distributed processing.
-

Chapter 8

Planning an Office Automation System

In chapter 7 we talked about finding where the information is in your organization and where it needs to go. That process should give you an initial picture of the types of equipment that you would like to have and how they should all tie together. This chapter will help to sharpen the focus on that picture. *

Of course, it isn't enough for you to put down on paper exactly what you need and how much you can get before the costs exceeds the benefits: so many word processors, so many facsimile machines, this technology, that topology, and so forth. For that, you need expert advice—preferably from your own staff or, failing that, from an outside consultant. If you usually deal with one data processing vendor and you have trust in him, his advice is also worth seeking.

You can't expect to design your own system. That's not what you are paid for and not what you were trained for. But you should feel that you can control the process, understand and guide the decisions, and defend your organization's interests. That is the purpose of the next two chapters. Indeed, that is the purpose of the whole book.

In this chapter, we will give you some guidelines for translating your understanding of the information needs of your organization into

---

*The tables and many of the ideas in this chapter are from an excellent publication by the National Bureau of Standards, Guidance on Requirements Analysis for Office Automation Systems (Washington, DC: U.S. Government Printing Office, National Bureau of Standards, December 1980).

an overall plan for an office automation system. In the next chapter, we take the final step: translating these office automation requirements into system requirements for a local network.

The process to be described in this chapter has three steps:

1. Define objectives.
2. Describe the system.
3. Determine communications needs.

As we proceed, you will notice that the discussion is useful in determining your data processing equipment needs. The focus of this book is on local area networks—on helping you procure them, incorporate them into your organization, and control their use and evolution. But, because the principles to be applied are general, they are also useful in the broader context that includes the devices that hook into this network.

DEFINE OBJECTIVES

By applying the principles described in chapter 7, you have a good idea of the current information needs of your organization—its production, storage, and uses. You can probably see several ways to improve the productivity of your "information workers." You are prepared to make capital investments if they are justified by the expected benefits. But first, you must get more specific. You must be able to answer in quantitative terms the question, "What is the information-movement and processing system supposed to do?"

It is best to begin by defining some productivity goals. The goals must be quantitative and relate to information creation, storage, transfer, and reporting. General categories include timeliness, responsiveness, convenience, and workload. The goals you set must be based on the situation you have today and where you feel improvements are needed.

For example, suppose it is important in your organization to get out reports or documents quickly and that these documents must usually be revised because of an internal review cycle. A productivity goal, then, would be to reduce revision typing time. Another example: Certain key professionals are the only ones in a position to produce certain briefing materials or reports, and this is draining too much of their time. A corresponding productivity goal would be to reduce professional effort required during the information-creation phase.

Remember, these goals must be stated quantitatively. Think in terms of how many documents need to be produced by how many people, the time it should take to prepare charts, and so forth.

FIGURE 8-1. TYPICAL LIST OF PRODUCTS.

---

1. Correspondence:	Letter
	Memorandum
	Message
2. Reports:	Management
	Trip
	Technical
	Incident
	Project Status
	Fiscal
	Personnel
	Weekly Activities
	Material Deficiency
	Training
3. Documents:	Statement of Work (SOW)
	Specifications
	Procurement Plan
	Program Management Directive
	Program Management Plan
	Letter Request
	Sole Source Justification
	Determination and Finding (D&F)
	Invitation for Bid
	Request for Proposal (RFP)
	EEO Certification
	Small Business Coordination
	Pre-Award Survey
	Model Contract
	Change Order
	Administrative Notice
	Source Selection Plan

Annual Call for Estimate
Obligation Authority (AO)
Procurement Directive
Delivery Order
Cost Estimate
Independent Cost Analysis (ICA)
Contract Funds Status Report (CFSR)
Staff Meeting Agenda (and Report)
Action Item List
Configuration Change Status Report
    (CCSR)
Engineering Change Proposal (ECP)
Quarterly Resources Report
System Safety Program Plan
Configuration Control Board Minutes
Data Management Report
Training Plan
Integrated Logistics Support Plan
    (ILSP)
Program Management System
    Checklist
Contract Management Systems
    Checklist
Military Construction Program
    Reporting
Site Survey Report
Environmental Assessment
Life-Cycle Cost Study
Phase-Out Plan

4. Forms:

Contract Data Requirements List
    (CDRL)
Security Classification Guide
Inspection and Acceptance Document
Data Item Description
Personnel Action Request
Time Card
Work Order Request
Security Monitor
Printing Request
Position Description
Purchase Request
Report of Survey

Travel Request
Military Order

5. Reviews/Briefings: Business Strategy Panel Meeting
Quarterly Financial Review
Periodic Program Review
Program Management Review (PMR)
Executive Management Review
  (EMR)
Resources Utilization Committee
  (RUC) Action
Financial Management Board Review
Division Advisory Group (DAG)
  Review
Scientific Advisory Board (SAB)
  Meeting
Command or Senior Officer Briefing
Internal Management Review

6. Audiovisual Aids: Vugraph
Briefing Text
Graphic Aid
35mm Slide
Briefing Board

At this stage, don't limit the number of things you look at. Consider all your "information products." Figure 8-1 can be used as a checklist. You should of course consider the feasibility and significance of your goals. Propose goals in practicable areas where there is room for significant improvement. If certain activities are already being accomplished efficiently, leave them be.

Finally, prioritize your goals. There are bound to be trade-offs in any system. Therefore, it is important to be clear up-front about the relative importance of things on your wish list.

DESCRIBE THE SYSTEM

Now you have some specific goals. The next thing to do is to list some options for moving closer to achieving those goals. As a manager, you know that not all improvements come from buying equipment. Consider three interrelated methods of achieving improvement: organizational, procedural, technological. Perhaps things are being done by the wrong group (organizational), or in the wrong way (procedural), or with inadequate equipment (technological).

Of course, these factors affect each other. A technological change may dictate an organizational change. For example, if it becomes quick and easy to produce charts at a new graphics terminal, then perhaps they should be produced by professionals rather than a support group.

Figure 8-2 gives some idea of how these three factors can be used to improve productivity.

FIGURE 8-2 System Design Model.

Organizational	Procedural	Technological
Accounting Department will be responsible for initial compilation of budget data.	Typing staff will prepare first drafts of key products using selectric typewriters with OCR fonts.	Electronic typewriters W/OCR fonts
Program Management Staff will be responsible for researching program information.	Math computations will be performed by the statistical research staff.	Desktop cassette dictation equipment
Program Management staff will replace the Accounting staff in the review of key products relating to grant applications.	Support staff will be designated as product distributors.	OCR reader
	Professional staff will provide first draft input through the use of dictation equipment.	Stand-alone Display Word Processors
	Final drafts will be microfilmed rather than filed.	Minicomputer
		Facsimile
		Microfilm Reader-Printers

Our focus is, of course, technological. We need to determine what additional equipment can be beneficial. We can group our options into four categories: input, production, output, and distribution. Figure 8-3 (pp. 106-11) lists representative equipment in each category, together with a description of benefits and drawbacks, and an estimate of productivity improvement. This will allow you to assess the impact of various pieces of equipment.

DETERMINE COMMUNICATIONS NEEDS

You know what information equipment you have. You have decided, at least tentatively, what creation, processing, and storage equipment is supposed to achieve in terms of productivity. The last element is the information-movement equipment, the local network. To be truly effective and efficient, your collection of equipment must become a system capable of moving information as well as creating, processing, and storing it.

Before you go out to buy your local network, you must specify your requirements, and these boil down, actually, to two considerations: compatibility and capacity.

Compatibility is the easier of the two to specify, but the harder to achieve. You simply need to determine which devices need to exchange data. For example, if you intend to combine data from an accounting system with text from a word processor, then there must be an electrical path from the accounting system to the word processor, and the word processor must be able to accept and process the data received.

The second part, *capacity,* is more difficult to pin down but, paradoxically, easier to satisfy. In fact, you don't need to be terribly accurate in estimating capacity! Local networks, by and large, have tremendous capacity; that is one of their chief advantages. For example, the National Bureau of Standards has a local network that uses a baseband cable, with a 1-Mbps data rate and CSMA/CD protocol. By today's standards, this is a system with modest capacity and performance characteristics. Over 200 devices in twenty buildings

FIGURE 8-3. Productivity Citings for Representative Equipment Types

These sample productivity improvement citings have been derived from representative sources available as of March 1, 1980. New technological developments are rapidly changing the productivity to be derived from the use of these representative equipment types. Therefore, the information needs to be continuously researched and updated.

INPUT PHASE

Equipment	Benefits	Drawbacks	Citing
Dictation	• Input is four times faster than longhand • Transcription is twice as fast as reading longhand or shorthand • Any secretary can transcribe • Priority work can be handled • 24-hour input is allowed	• Clarity of thought and expression is required • Pre-organization of material by dictator is necessary • Many originators resist dictation	• 6.25%–12% time savings/day—Herbert M. Kaplan, *Words*, International Word Processing Association, June–July 1980, pp. 40-43.
Electronic Typewriter with OCR Font	• Correction time is reduced • Input via OCR reader into production equipment is possible	• No text editing is possible • No storage capacity is available • Input into production equipment is off-line	• See Optical Character Recognition citing
Optical Character Recognition	• Every typewriter with an OCR font can be a low level input device for text editing and data manipulation • Re-keyboarding of input text/data is eliminated • Production equipment is freed for word or data processing • Work distribution is enhanced	• Generally only a limited number of fonts can be read • Scanning errors are possible • Specific input formats may be required • Accuracy depends upon ribbon, strike, paper, and other variables	• 600% increase in throughput, Compuscan sales literature, AW-5B-018.0

Equipment	Benefits	Drawbacks	Citings
Personal (Professional) Terminal	• Data entry, access, and retrieval time can be reduced • Paper and supplies can be saved through electronic capture of keystrokes • Can be expanded, reconfigured, or networked as applications expand and new requirements evolve	• Training is required • CPU downtime can affect the use of the terminal • Response degradation may occur during peak periods	• 50% productivity rise- Emerick G. Zouks, *Business Week*, April 7, 1980, pp. 81-82.

PRODUCTION PHASE

Equipment	Benefits	Drawbacks	Citings
Blind Automatic Word Processor	• Correction time is reduced • Light-change text editing is handled	• Text editing functions are limited • Large amounts of text cannot be manipulated • Storage may be limited	• Average 48%-69% productivity improvement if used for original and revision typing; average 69%-98% if used for revision only; NARS standards
Stand-alone Display Text Editors	• Extensive text editing is easily handled • Input and formatting is facilitated by a CRT • Saves paper and supplies through electronic capture of keystrokes	• Some are unprogrammable • Large data bases may not be manipulated • Storage may be limited	• Average 75%-133% productivity improvement if used for original and revision typing; average 104%-181% if used for revision only; NARS standards

FIGURE 8-3 (cont'd) Productivity Citings for Representative Equipment Types

Equipment	Benefits	Drawbacks	Citings
Shared Logic Word Processor	• Extensive text editing is easily handled • Input and formatting is facilitated by a CRT • Saves paper and supplies through electronic capture of keystrokes • Different tasks may be performed at the same time • Some are programmable by the user	• CPU downtime can be a problem • Specially trained personnel may be necessary to administer the system • Response degradation may occur during peak periods • System backup may be limited	• Average 84%-89% productivity improvement if used for original and revision typing; average 115%-122% if used for revision only; NARS standards
Minicomputer	• Can be expanded, reconfigured, or networked as applications expand and new requirements evolve • Performs many different tasks at the same time • Can support simultaneous users • Is programmable • Paper and supplies can be saved through electronic capture of keystrokes	• Early obsolescence on large investment is a risk • System backup may be limited • CPU downtime can be a problem • Response degradation may occur during peak periods	• Same statistics as for shared logic word processors • Data processing figure totally dependent on each application
Data Processing System	• Handles many applications • Is programmable • Can be expanded, reconfigured, or networked as applications expand and new requirements evolve • Performs many different tasks at the same time • Can support a large number of users • Handles large amounts of text or data	• CPU downtime can be a problem • Specially trained personnel may be necessary to administer the system • May be susceptible to response degradation during peak periods • System backup may be limited • Techniques and procedures usually are alien to the office environment	• Same statistics as for shared logic word processors • Data processing figure totally dependent on each application

OUTPUT PHASE

Equipment	Benefits	Drawbacks	Citings
Word Processing Impact Printer	• High quality print is produced • Carbon copies can be created • Automatic single sheet feeder or continuous form paper may be used	• Changing printwheels can be time-consuming • Inserting paper may be required	• 15 to 55 characters per second burst speed, *Datapro Reports on Word Processing*, April 1980 • 148-533% faster than electric typewriter capability
Word Processing Non-Impact Printer	• High quality print is produced • Automatically feeds paper • Typestyles are changed electronically within the printer	• Usually prints no carbon copies	• 77 to 92 characters per second burst speed, *Datapro Reports on Word Processing*, April 1980 • 770-918% faster than electric typewriter capability
Data Processing Printer	• Prints at high speeds • Carbon copies can be created • Usually incorporates an automatic paper feed	• Print quality is usually unacceptable for word processing output	• 40-120 characters per second (matrix), *Auerbach Computer Technology Reports #31*, 1978, p. 13 • 1,184-3,554% faster than electric typewriter capability • 150-2,000 lines per minute (line), *Auerbach Computer Technology Reports #31*, 1978, p. 13 • 4,813-6,417% faster than electric typewriter capability
Photocomposers	• Word processors may serve as a means of keyboarding for preparing photocomposer input • User can save between 30-40% in the final required number of pages • OCRs may be used to generate photocomposer tapes • Document preparation time may be decreased	• May be less expensive to procure this service from outside vendors • Compatibility with other systems may be a problem	• 20-80 lines per minute, *Datapro Reports on Office Systems*, September 1979 • 641-2,566% faster than electric typewriter capability

Figure 8-3 (cont.)

Equipment	Benefits	Drawbacks	Citings
Micrographics	• Recording on microfilm consumes as little as 2% of the space occupied by the same records on paper • Only seconds are involved in retrieving one of a million records filed within reach of a seated operator • Duplicate microfilm files kept off premises to protect against loss of vital information • Magnetic-tape data are made readable on microfilm in a fraction of the time required for printing out on paper • Microfilm records retention cost is considerably lower than paper records systems	• Archive quality of film images is questionable • Quality control and inspection procedures must be maintained during the filming, processing, and storage activities • Complexities exist when indexing for automated retrieval • High costs may be associated with conversion of existing paper files to microform images	• 25% (Commander Lloyd C. Burger)-62% (Reuben Donnelly) access/retrieval time savings, *Modern Office Procedures*, May 1977, p. 60

DISTRIBUTION PHASE

Equipment	Benefits	Drawbacks	Citings
Intelligent Copiers	• Document storage can be reduced • Speed of document communications can be enhanced • Scope of document communications can be enhanced • Acts as a convenience copier	• Copier may be used as a printing press with increased per page costs • Potential exists for excess copying • Potential exists for non-business copying	• 75-600 characters/second transmission speed, IBM 6670 literature (G54 1006) • When 600 cps compared to 2 days for mail to arrive, 3927 times faster for page with 50 lines (65 characters/line)

110

Equipment	Benefits	Drawbacks	Citing
Facsimile (FAX)	• Electronically sends text, graphic data, photographs, drawings or charts with little difficulty • Documents transfer much faster than mail, messenger, etc.	• Line costs are relatively high • Compatibility with receiving device must exist • Sizes of sending and receiving documents are limited • Certain devices require station-to-station coordination • Quality of received documents may not be acceptable	• 30 sec- 6 min. to transmit 8½ x 11 page, *Datapro Reports on Office Systems #2*, June 1980 • When 6 min. compared to 2 days for mail to arrive, 480 times faster
Executive Telephones	• Reduces staff time in using the telephone • Provides arithmetic capabilities	• Difficult to cost justify	• No citing available
Word Processing Data Processing System with Communications Feature	• Increased speed of document or data communications	• Possible compatibility problems with mainframe or minicomputer	• 40% reduction in dissemination time, *Report on Electronic Mail*, 4th Quarter 1978, Yankee Group, p. 13

Note on equipment table: Several items are listed here that we have not discussed before.

- Blind Automatic Word Processor—this is a unit without a display, with text usually stored on magnetic cards or tape.
- Executive Telephone—a combination telephone and calculator. Features may include call pickup, automatic dialing, one-line display, calculating, clocking, and appointment calendaring.

Having picked some candidate equipment, you need to look at the cost. You have to judge the worth or benefit of any item compared to its cost. Once you have done that, you can boil the list down to those things you are prepared to buy. This is a preliminary list, but at least it gives you and any potential vendor a clear idea of your requirements.

are connected, with the most distant span separated by 1.5 kilometers. This is not a prototype or experimental system; it is in daily use by a staff with far greater data processing needs than the average office. Yet, the utilization of the network's information movement capacity is under 2 percent!

So, for this part, don't worry about trying to make very precise estimates. All that a network designer needs to determine the size of the system is a general idea of the workload and performance demands on the network.

Figure 8-4 summarizes the information needed to design a network. Again, you do not need exact numbers for this checklist; rough estimates will be sufficient.

The first thing to do is to list each type of information exchange that can take place. Make a matrix listing all the devices on the network at both the top and the side of the matrix. Each square of the matrix represents a possible communication path. Check those that will

FIGURE 8-4. Capacity Checklist

For Each Type of Information Exchange:
- Initiator Device and Location
- Responder Device and Location

For File Transfers:
- Amount of Data for Transfer
- Time Allotted for Transfer

For Transactions:
- Amount of Data Requested
- Response Time

For Total System:
- Average Loading
- Peak Loading
- Performance Goals

Future Growth:
- Number of Devices
- File Size
- Added Functions

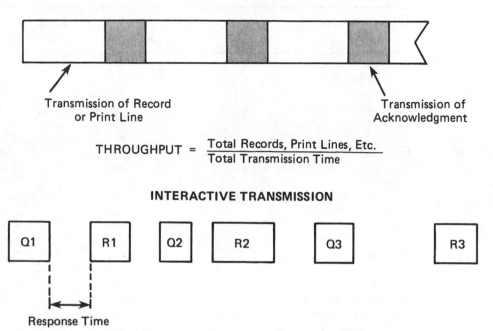

BATCH TRANSMISSION

Transmission of Record
or Print Line

Transmission of
Acknowledgment

$$\text{THROUGHPUT} = \frac{\text{Total Records, Print Lines, Etc.}}{\text{Total Transmission Time}}$$

INTERACTIVE TRANSMISSION

Q1   R1   Q2   R2   Q3   R3

Response Time

Figure 8-5 The performance criteria of a system depend upon the function you want the system to perform. Some information-movement functions involve the one-way transfer of large amounts of data. Other functions involve frequent interaction between stations. A manager evaluating a system for file transfer should be more concerned with throughput. A manager evaluating an interactive system should be more concerned with response time.

be used. For any information exchange, one device is the initiator, the other the responder. The types can be listed in that fashion.

Information exchanges can be grouped into two broad categories: file transfer and transaction. A *file transfer* is primarily a one-way movement of data, such as the transfer of a word processing file to a printer or an image to a facsimile machine. *Transactions* are typically responses to inquiries or requests for data. In the first case, you are more concerned with throughput: the amount of data to be transferred in a given time. In the second case, you are more concerned with response time: how long it takes to get an item after it is requested.

Of course, some of your information exchange types will not fit completely into either category. Since this whole process need not be exact, just put each entry in the category that seems more appropriate.

Figure 8-6 will give you an idea of the kind of workload that can be generated by various devices on a local network. These estimates

FIGURE 8-6. Workload Generated from Each Source Type.

Type of Source	Peak Data Rate (KBPS)	Duty Factor (%)
Heat/Vent/Air Conditioning/ Alarm/Security	0.1	100
Line Printer	19.2	50-90
File Server/Block Transfer	20,000	0.1
File Server/File Transfer	100	10-30
Mail Server	100	30-50
Information Server/Calendar	9.6	1.5
Information Server/Decision Support	56	20-40
Word Processor	9.6	1-5
Data Entry Terminal	9.6	0.1-1.0
Data Enquiry Terminal	64	10-30
Program Development	9.6	5-20
Laser Printer	256	20-50
Facsimile	9.6	5-20
Voice/Immediate	64	20-40
Voice/Store and Forward	32	30-50
Video/Noncompressed	30,000	50-90
Video/Freeze Frame	64	50-90
Video/Compressed	400	20-40
Graphics/Noncompressed	256	1-10
Graphics/Compressed	64	10-30
Optical Character Reader	2.4	50-90
Gateway	1,000	0.1-1.0
Host/0.5 MIPS	128	20-40
Host/5 MIPS	1,000	20-30

were developed by a local network study group of the Institute of Electrical and Electronics Engineers.

Next, you need to look at total demand for capacity. On the average, how many of these information exchanges will be taking place at a time? What is the peak? There is typically one period during the day when the load on the system peaks: A lot of people and machines are using the network. For file transfers, you can now add things up to get some idea of overall throughput demand on the network. For transactions, it is better to try to express your needs in terms of a performance goal. For example, for a certain type of transaction, you might specify that you want 90 percent of the transactions to have a response within three seconds.

Finally, you need to look at future growth. If your organization is growing, you will someday want to buy some new devices. Your total file size will grow. You may add new functions to the network. The network should be designed to accommodate growth. Given the capabilities of today's local networks, you should be able to install a network now that will not need to be replaced later. If you do it right, you'll do it once.

THINGS TO REMEMBER

- Before you go out to buy a local network, develop a plan for the system that the network is called upon to support.
- Define the objectives of the system. What productivity goals are appropriate and have high payoff for your organization?
- Based on those goals, describe a system of reasonable cost to meet those goals.
- Based on that system description, determine your communications needs in terms of compatibility and capacity. The capacity requirements can be stated as rough estimates.

Chapter 9

Buying
A Local Network

Having gone through the process of planning a system, you are now in a position to translate your needs into a statement of network requirements. Chapter 8 developed your requirements from a user or application point of view. That should help you answer the question, "What is the system supposed to do?" The next step is to answer the question, "What features must the local network have to meet my system requirements?"

There are two points to keep in mind as you go through this chapter. First, the caveat of chapter 8 applies. We are not trying to teach you how to design your own network; we just want you to be able to hold your own in dealing with the experts and would-be experts. Second, the emphasis is still on *what* the network will do, not *how* the network will do it. The *what* is the customer's responsibility; the *how* is the vendor's responsibility. Don't make the mistake of precluding a cost-effective solution by telling the vendor how to do his job.

GENERAL SELECTION CRITERIA

In the first part of this chapter, we give you some general selection criteria to keep in mind as you consider various vendors. These are the

Figure 9-1. Vendor Selection Criteria.

- TOTAL COST

- MEETS REQUIREMENTS

- EXPANDABLE INCREMENTALLY IN COST

- CAPABLE OF INTERFACING WITH EQUIPMENT SUPPLIED BY MULTI-PLE VENDORS

- EASE OF:
    - INSTALLATION
    - MAINTENANCE
    - RECONFIGURATION
    - INTERCONNECTION

features that you should look for and that should allow you to compare offerings from different vendors.

The first criterion, of course, is cost. If the cost exceeds what you perceive as the expected savings in increased productivity, then the system isn't worth the price.

Second, the network has to meet your requirements. You've developed a picture of what you want from chapters 7 and 8. Of course, there are always compromises, but the system must match the basic picture of what you need. Related to this picture is the concept that the network should be expandable with only incremental cost. That is to say, if you put in now what you can afford, there should not be a big retrofit job later to expand the system. This will allow you to start small, at low risk, and gradually expand the network to meet more and more of your requirements.

Along with expandability, you need reliability. The system should be designed to prevent total network failure. Otherwise you may end up losing productivity rather than gaining it.

The network should be capable of interfacing with equipment supplied by more than one vendor. We will explore this issue at the end of the chapter.

You want a network that is easy to install, maintain, and occasionally reconfigure. Flexibility is important. You want to be able to connect your equipment to the network easily, with no impact on your hardware or software.

SPECIFIC NETWORK REQUIREMENTS*

Let's consider specifically what you will require of a network. Much of the information was assembled in chapter 8, and a knowledgeable consultant or vendor can work with that. The purpose of this section is to give you a better idea of what to ask for, a checklist of what has to be provided before you sign on the dotted line.

We can group our concerns into five areas:

- Services
- Traffic
- Reliability
- Growth
- Installation, maintenance, and training.

Services

The functions performed by the network that are the most visible to users and management are referred to as *network services*.

A primary consideration in developing network services is the physical network environment. Is the network all in one building or spread over several? If the latter, must the buildings be linked together? Where is the equipment located? What space is available for network components? What false ceilings, conduits, and buried cable runs exist for wiring? Are there any special environmental problems? All these things must be considered.

Next, what type of equipment will be supported? This consideration leads to the question of interfaces. As we mentioned, RS-232-C is a common electrical interface and should suffice for most terminals and computers. Other devices, such as printers and tape drives, may require other interfaces. It is important to note that only those resources that need to be shared should be on the network. For example, if you have a special plotter that must be driven by the software in one and only one computer, then hook the plotter to the computer—don't make them communicate over the network.

There is also the software interface to consider. For example, you must consider what protocols are provided to allow terminals to communicate with a variety of computers. If you have several

---

*This section is based on an excellent National Bureau of Standards publication, *Guidelines for the Selection of Local Area Computer Networks* (Washington, DC: U.S. Government Printing Office, National Bureau of Standards, July 1981).

computers that can communicate using the X.25 standard, then the network needs to support that.

Next, consider the type of information to be transmitted over the network. This is the whole point of having a network. For data, your primary concern here is one of compatibility. Given the types of equipment you will have and the types of data to be transmitted, the network must provide whatever transport and presentations protocols are needed to permit full connectability.

Security and privacy are a concern. When there are multiple user groups who have access to the network, the network must provide means for isolating information and restricting access to it. Similarly, unauthorized users should be kept off the network altogether.

Another concern is remote communications. You may wish to link two installations by a satellite data channel. Or, you may want to augment your in-house processing capability with outside services, available over a packet-switching network, such as Telenet or Tymnet. You may also wish to provide dial-in ports so that members of your organization who are traveling can enter the network from anywhere in the country.

Finally, there is one service that is absolutely essential to the successful operation of a network: network control and monitoring. An operator must be able to view certain network statistics, including:

- Number of users connected
- Amount and type of traffic
- Error rates
- Hardware status

Summary reports of these statistics should be provided. "Real-time" status may also be useful.

The operator should be able to control the network: make connections, shut down stations, and so forth.

Traffic

The network must have the capability to meet the expected traffic load. This was explored in chapter 8. Throughput and response-time requirements must be specified. Especially important are peak-load requirements.

For bus or ring networks, a good rule of thumb is that the network should have ten times the required capacity. For example, if after adding up all the peak throughput requirements from all devices, you come up with a figure of 100 Kbps, then the data rate of the cable should be at least 1 Mbps.

For PABX systems, a different rule is more useful. Here, you are concerned with *blocking factor*. This is an expression that refers to the number of devices that can be simultaneously active on the network. For example, if you have 200 terminals and computers hooked up and expect that during a peak hour, 100 devices will be in use, then the PABX must support at least this 50-percent utilization. Incidentally, a PABX that allows all devices to be in use at one time is called *nonblocking*. It is unlikely that you will need this rather expensive capability.

Reliability

The network must be available to its users a very high percentage of the time, and there must be a long period of time between component and total network failure and a minimal period before repairs are completed. A useful measure of reliability is the *mean time between failures (MTBF)*. Here are some representative numbers. For the transmission medium, which includes the cable or wire, amplifiers, taps, and so on, an MTBF of 175,000 hours is reasonable. For intelligent network devices, such as switches or interface units for attaching devices, an MTBF of 30,000 hours is a good goal.

Another aspect of reliability is the *error rate* of transmitted information. This is usually expressed as the rate of bit errors. There are two types of error rates to be concerned about: undetected and detected. Undetected errors are very undesirable. An undetected error means that an error was introduced and you didn't know about it until after the error was discovered the hard way: The numbers didn't balance, or somebody didn't get a paycheck. Detected errors are those discovered by the network. The network then automatically takes steps to correct them, usually through retransmission. Detected errors are not as bad, but they do cause unnecessary overhead in the network.

Good reliability values are a detected-error rate of 1 bit in 10^9 and an undetected-error rate of 1 bit in 10^{12}. Detected-error rates are easily monitored. Undetected-error rates must be estimated from off-line tests using artificial traffic.

Growth

Even if you had all the money you need, you cannot expect to satisfy all your local network needs once and for all.

For example, you may anticipate that your word processing staff will double in the next three years. It must be easy to attach these additional stations to the network, with no disruption of network operations. Also, the network must have the capability to handle the increased traffic generated by the new stations.

New types of applications or devices might also be added to the network—for example, a facsimile machine. This will require new protocols. If such growth is to be possible, the network hardware and software must be capable of easily accommodating new protocols.

Installation, Maintenance, and Training

The preceding criteria had to do with the capability and capacity of the network you are going to procure. This section speaks to an equally important consideration—the service provided by the vendor. Installation, of course, is a service you expect from your vendor. This is not a simple task. First, the vendor must plan, with your cooperation, the layout of the network. This includes the physical placement of all cable and wiring and the location of all network components. In the case of cable, these include taps, splitters, and amplifiers. The vendor must assure that the layout meets all fire and other building codes.

Following installation, maintenance of the network is an ongoing responsibility, a responsibility divided between you and the vendor. How that responsibility is divided varies from one situation to the next. What is presented in the next few paragraphs is just an example.

For the network hardware, the customer has the following responsibilities:

- Maintain a permanent survey of the network through the use of logging files and traffic statistics.
- When a problem occurs, perform diagnostics to attempt to localize the fault, using vendor-supplied test equipment and diagnostic software.
- When the fault is localized, reconfigure the network, if possible, to provide continued service.
- Assist the vendor in network checkout after failure correction by the vendor.

Customer personnel will require training from the vendor to perform these tasks.

The vendor's hardware maintenance responsibilities are:

- Cross-check customer diagnostics, if necessary.
- Replace failed components. (To minimize lost service time, faulty components are replaced rather than repaired.)
- Perform network checkout after failure correction.

If the network includes substantial software, which is likely, software maintenance becomes quite complex. This should be left entirely to the vendor.

Closely related to maintenance is training. As we mentioned, some customer personnel need training to participate in maintenance activities. One or more individuals will need to be trained in network-management functions. Network management includes such things as user authorization, network configuration, and priority definition.

Users, in general, should require little or no training. The application user should, at most, have to learn a log-on procedure. Beyond that the network should be transparent to the user.

TYPE OF NETWORK

A key decision in your network procurement process is the type of network to buy. Your major choices are:

- PABX
- Baseband bus
- Broadband bus
- Ring

You need to consider all the selection criteria we've mentioned in making your choice. But the two most important ones, for deciding network type, are *cost* and *capacity*.

Figure 9-2, based on a recent study by the Institute of Electrical and Electronics Engineers, gives you some idea of relative costs. Rings, not shown on the chart, would be about the same as baseband bus. As you can see, the study showed that baseband and broadband were very close, with a small advantage to broadband in larger installations. The PABX is considerably cheaper. Of course, prices are changing rapidly—in general, they are dropping—so you should get budgetary estimates from a variety of vendors. But the conclusion to be drawn is unlikely to change: For most applications, the PABX is the best choice of a local network because it provides the most commonly used capabilities at the lowest cost.

But that guideline may not be true for your installation. There is that other criterion—capacity. The throughput of the PABX is limited. Currently, an upper limit of about 56 Kbps per device is typical, and the total peak throughput is also limited. Higher limits can be achieved with a bus or ring.

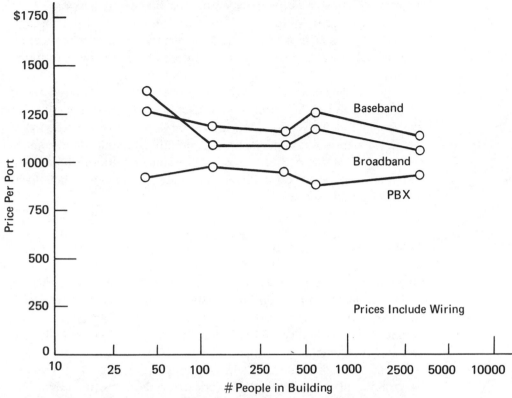

COST OF VARIOUS DATA OPTIONS 1 Port Per User (19.2–56KB)

Baseband

Broadband

PBX

Prices Include Wiring

Price Per Port

People in Building

Figure 9-2 This chart gives a proportional relationship between the size and price of broadband, baseband, and PBX local networks. Of course, price isn't everything. Each type of system has certain operational advantages and disadvantages that must also be considered.

Other factors come into play. For example, if you already have a CATV installation, you may avoid a major part of the installation cost for a broadband bus by using the existing cable.

Be flexible. Consider various types. Don't talk to just one vendor.

TYPE OF VENDOR

One final point to consider is the type of vendor. There is a broad spectrum here, but we will group them into two categories to clarify the issue: the network vendor and the data processing vendor.

The network vendor's primary business is to sell local networks. Typically, network vendors are small independents or subsidiaries. Two

123

examples, discussed in appendix A, are AMDAX and Rolm. The network vendor makes his money from the sale of the network.

The data processing vendor, on the other hand, is in business to sell data processing equipment. A local network is a means of meeting a customer's need for linking together the equipment he buys from the vendor.

Which type of vendor should you go with? If you already have or are planning to procure most of your data processing equipment from one vendor and that vendor offers a local network, it makes sense to get the network from the same vendor—it simplifies maintenance responsibilities. If, for one reason or another, the situation doesn't hold, then you might be better off with a local network vendor, since local networks are his specialty.

THINGS TO REMEMBER

There are some general selection criteria to keep in mind when trying to make a local network decision. The most important are total cost and that the network meet your requirements. Other criteria are expandability, reliability, ability to handle a variety of equipment, and ease of management.

The network must meet some specific requirements. These can be grouped in the following categories: services, traffic, reliability, growth, installation and maintenance.

Glossary

This glossary presents technical and operational words in an easily understood form. We hope you will find it to be one of the most valuable portions of the book.

access method. This is an IBM term with a precise meaning. It refers to specific kinds of communications software which includes some protocols for exchanging data, constructing files, and other functions. This term is used in the local network context to refer to the method of determining which device has access to the transmission medium at any instant. CSMA/CD is an example of an access method.

ACF. See *Advanced Communications Function.*

ACK. A positive acknowledgment control character. This character is exchanged between system components when data have been received without error. This control character is also used as an affirmative response for setting up a communications exchange.

acoustic coupler. The portion of a modem that physically holds a telephone handset in two rubber cups. The cups house a small microphone and speaker which "talk" and "listen" to the telephone handset.

A/D converter. A device that converts analog signals to digital.

ADCCP. Advanced Data Communications Control Procedure, a bit-oriented ANSI standard communications protocol. It is a link-layer protocol.

Advanced Communications Function. An IBM program package to allow sharing of computer resources through communications links. Supports SNA.

Advanced Communications Service. A large data communications network developed by AT&T.

alphanumeric. Characters made up of letters and numbers. Usually contrasted to graphics or video.

analog. In common use, this term refers to transmission methods developed to transmit voice signals. These methods were designed only for the bandwidth of the human voice (up to about 3 KHz). This limits their capability to pass high-speed digital signals.

ANSI. American National Standards Institute. Develops and publishes standards for codes, alphabets, and signaling schemes.

application layer. The seventh (top) layer of the OSI architecture. Not described in detail by the architecture. This layer determines the interface of the device with the user.

ARQ. A control code that calls for the retransmission of a block of data.

ASCII. American Standard Code for Information Exchange. More correctly known as USASCII because of some change in recent versions. A method of coding digital signals. The ASCII character contains seven bits; an eighth parity bit is often added.

ASR. Automatic send-receive. A term left over from teleprinters that punched messages on paper tape. Now, it is sometimes used to mean any terminal that has a storage capability.

asynchronous. A method of transmission in which the time intervals between characters are not required to be equal. Start and stop bits are added to coordinate the transfer of characters.

attenuated. Reduced: "The signal was attenuated by the high resistance in the line." Amplifiers and better cables are the answer to attenuation.

background program (mode). A program that performs its functions while the operator is working with a second, different program. Communications programs often operate in the background mode on word processors. They can receive messages while the operator is processing words. The messages are stored for later display.

bandwidth. The range of frequencies a circuit will pass. Analog circuits typically have a bandwidth limited to that of the human voice (about 3 KHz). The square waves of digital signals can be distorted by inadequate bandwidth. The faster the digital signal transmission rate, the greater the bandwidth requirement. Fiber-optic and broadband cables have excellent bandwidth.

baseband. Transmission of signals without modulation. In a baseband local network, digital signals (1s and 0s) are inserted directly onto the cable as voltage pulses. The entire bandwidth of the cable is consumed by the signal. This scheme does not allow frequency division multiplexing.

baud. A measure of transmission speed. The reciprocal of the time duration of the shortest signal element in a transmission. In RS-232-C ASCII, the signaling element is one bit.

Baudot code. A coding scheme for data transmission using a five-bit (five-level) code. Still used in older communications systems. The code known today as "Baudot" was really written by Donald Murray and replaced the older Baudot scheme. It is more correctly known as the Murray code. It is also referred to as CCITT alphabet number 2.

BCD. Binary-coded decimal. A coding scheme using a six-bit (six-level) code.

BDLC. Burroughs Data-Link Control. A bit-oriented protocol related to HDLC.

Bell 103. A modem protocol using four tones for full-duplex operation over standard telephone lines. Usually limited to 300 baud.

Bell 113. A modem protocol identical to Bell 103.

Bell 202. A modem protocol using two tones for half-duplex transmission. Maximum speed on dialed telephone lines is 1200 baud. The mark tone is 1200 Hz, and the space tone is 2200 Hz.

Bell 212. A dual-mode modem protocol featuring full-duplex transmission at speeds up to 300 baud using the 103 protocol or up to 1200 baud using a phase-shifted carrier. Not compatible with 202-type devices.

benchmark. A test program used to determine system speed and performance.

bisync. Binary Synchronous protocol. An IBM byte-oriented, link-layer communications protocol that is widely used. They are trying to replace it with SDLC.

bit. Smallest unit of information. In digital signaling, this commonly refers to a change in state between a 0 and a 1.

block. A number of characters transmitted as a group.

BNA. Burroughs Network Architecture.

bps. Bits per second.

broadband. A term used to refer to transmission media capable of passing wide-bandwidth signals. Usually classed as capable of data speeds of 19.2 Kbps or greater. In the local-network context, *broadband* refers to the use of frequency-multiplexed cable. Digital signals are passed through a modem and transmitted over one of the frequency bands of the cable.

BSC. See *bisync.*

buffer. A temporary storage space. Data may be stored in a buffer before they are transmitted and as they are received. A buffer may be used to compensate between the differences in the speed of transmission and the speed of processing.

bus. A transmission medium, usually coaxial fiber-optic cable. This term is usually associated with networks in the tree topology.

byte. A group of eight bits.

carrier. **1.** A radio frequency or lightwave that is transmitted over a cable and modulated with a signal. **2.** A company that provides transmission services. See *common carrier*.

CATV. Community-antenna television. Based on broadband coaxial-cable technology.

CBX. Computer branch exchange. A type of PABX. See *PABX*.

CCITT. Consultative Committee of International Telephone and Telegraph. A committee of the United Nations that develops and publishes international standards.

central retransmission facility. See *frequency converter*.

character. One letter, number, or special code.

channel. A communications path. A channel may be a physical link or a logical path described between two communicating units.

circuit switching. A method of communicating in which a dedicated communications path is established between two devices, bandwidth is guaranteed, and delay is essentially limited to propagation time. The telephone system uses circuit switching.

coaxial cable. An electrical-transmission cable with a center conductor and an outer electrical shield. Used in both broadband and baseband systems. Broadband cable has better shielding than baseband cable.

codec. Coder-decoder. Transforms analog voice into a digital bit stream (coder) and digital signals into analog voice (decoder) using PCM.

common carrier. A transmission company (such as the telephone company) that serves the general public.

communications controller. A programmable computer "front end" in the IBM SNA network.

contention. The condition when two stations attempt to use the same channel at the same time.

control character. A character used for special signaling. Often not printed or displayed, but causing special functions such as the movement of paper in a printer, the blanking of a display screen, or "handshaking" between communicating devices to control the flow of data.

cps. Characters per second.

CPU. Central processing unit. The functional "brain" of a computer. The element that does the actual adding and subtracting of 0s and 1s that is essential to computing.

CRC. Cyclic redundancy check.

CRT. Cathode ray tube. A video screen.

cross-talk. The spillover of a signal from one channel to another. In data communications it is very disruptive. Usually, careful adjustment of the circuits will eliminate cross-talk.

CSMA/CD. Carrier-sense multiple-access collision detection. A network-access technique by means of which stations sense the absence of a carrier on the medium and begin to transmit. If two stations transmit simultaneously, they detect the collision and cease transmitting. Each waits a period of time determined by special noninterference techniques before initiating transmission again.

current loop. An electrical interface that is sensitive to current changes rather than voltage swings. Used with older (often Baudot-encoded) teleprinter equipment.

cursor. The point of light indicating the place on the video screen where the next character will appear.

cyclic redundancy check (CRC). A numeric value derived from the bits in a message. The transmitting station uses one of several formulas to produce a number that is attached to the message. The receiving station applies the same formula and should derive the same number. If the numbers are not the same, an error condition is declared.

D/A. Digital-to-analog converter. Changes digital pulses into analog signals.

Data Access Protocol. A specialized protocol used by Digital Equipment Corporation.

data-flow control. A communications layer in SNA that creates and responds to outgoing and incoming messages.

data-link control. A communications layer in SNA that manages the physical data circuits.

data-link layer. See *link layer.*

data set. **1.** A file, a "set" of data. **2.** The name the telephone company often uses for a modem.

DB-25. The designation of a standard plug-and-jack set used in RS-232-C wiring: twenty-five pin connectors, thirteen pins in the top row and twelve in the bottom row.

DCA. Distributed Communications Architecture. Developed by Sperry-Univac.

DCE. Data communications equipment. A common designation for communications equipment such as computers and modems. Uses a female DB-25 chassis plug.

DDD. Direct distance dialing. Use of the common long-distance telephone system.

DDCMP. See *Digital Data Communications Message Protocol.*

DECnet. A local area network from Digital Equipment Corporation with extensive network management capabilities.

delay. In addition to the common meaning of a pause in activity, delay can also be a kind of distortion on a communications circuit. Delay is the property of an electrical circuit which slows down and distorts high-frequency signals. Devices called equalizers slow down the lower frequencies and "equalize" the signal.

dial-up line. A communications circuit established by dialing a destination over a commercial telephone system.

digital. In common use, on-off signaling. Signals consist of 0s and 1s instead of a great multitude of analog-modulated frequencies.

Digital Data Communications Message Protocol (DDCMP). A Digital Equipment Corporation byte-oriented, link-layer protocol used to transmit messages over a communications line.

distortion. Any change to the transmitted signal. May be caused by cross-talk, delay, attenuation, or other factors.

Distributed Systems Architecture (DSA). A Honeywell architecture that conforms to the Open System Interconnection model proposed by the ISO. It supports X.25 for packet switching and X.21 for packet-switched and circuit-switched network protocols.

DTE. Data terminal equipment. A common designation for data processing equipment such as printers, terminals, and computers. Uses a male DB-25 chassis plug.

dual cable. A type of broadband cable system in which two separate cables are used, one for transmission and one for reception.

duplex. **1.** In communications circuits, the ability to transmit and receive at the same time. Also referred to as *full-duplex*. *Half-duplex* circuits can receive only or transmit only. **2.** In terminals, a choice of a display of locally generated characters or a display of echoed characters.

EBCDIC. Extended Binary-Coded Decimal Interchange Code. An eight-bit code used primarily on IBM business systems.

echoplex. A method of transmission in which characters are echoed from the distant end and the echoes are presented on the terminal. Provides a constant check of the communications circuit. See *full-duplex*.

echo suppressor. A device used to eliminate the echo effect of long-distance voice transmission circuits. These suppressors must be disabled for full-duplex data transmission. The modem answer tones turn the suppressors off automatically.

EIA. Electronic Industries Association.

emulation. Simulation of a system, function, or program.

EPBX. Electronic private branch exchange. See *PABX*.

equalization. Balancing of a circuit so that it passes all frequencies with equal efficiency.

Ethernet. A baseband local-area network marketed by Xerox and developed jointly by Xerox, Digital Equipment Corporation, and Intel.

facsimile (fax). The transmission of page images by a system that is concerned with patterns of light and dark rather than with specific characters. Older systems use analog signals. Newer devices use digital signals and may interact with computers and other digital devices.

FCC. Federal Communications Commission.

field. A particular position within a message frame. Positions are labeled as the control field, flag field, and so on. Bits in a particular message have a meaning for stations on the network.

foreign exchange. Not francs and pounds, but rather a telephone line that represents a local number in a calling area quite removed from its actual termination. If your office is in the suburbs, but many of your customers are in the city, you might have a foreign exchange line with a city telephone office.

four-wire circuit. A transmission arrangement where two half-duplex circuits (two wires each) are combined to make one full-duplex circuit.

frame. A group of bits that includes the message and address information.

frequency-agile modem (FAM). A modem used on some broadband systems that can shift frequencies so it can communicate with stations in different dedicated bands.

frequency converter. In broadband cable systems, the device that translates between the transmitting and receiving frequencies. Also known generically as a *head end.*

frequency-division multiplexing. A technique for combining many signals on one circuit by separating them in frequency.

frequency-shift keying (FSK). A transmission method using two different frequencies that are shifted to represent the digital 0s and 1s. Used in some common modems.

frequency translator. See *frequency converter.*

FSK. See *frequency-shift keying.*

full-duplex. The ability to talk both ways over a communications link at the same time.

functional-management layer. Formats presentations in SNA.

gateway. A device that connects two systems, especially if the systems use different protocols. For example, a gateway is needed to connect two independent local networks or to connect a local network to a long-haul network.

ground. An electrically neutral contact point.

half-duplex. **1.** Alternating transmissions. Each station can either transmit or receive, not both simultaneously. **2.** In terminals, used to describe the condition when a terminal displays its own transmissions instead of a distant-end echo.

handshaking. Exchange of control codes or specific characters to control the data flow.

HDLC. High-Level Data-Link Control. A comprehensive standard developed by the International Standards Organization (ISO). It is a bit-oriented link-layer protocol.

high-speed modem. A modem operating between 2400 and 9600 bps. See *wideband, low-speed,* and *medium-speed modem.*

HYPERchannel. A high-speed local-area network scheme from Network Systems Corporation (NSC). The HYPERchannel manages the physical, link-control, and networking layers in the communications system. It is designed to allow computers from other major manufacturers to communicate with IBM systems.

Hz (Hertz). Cycles per second.

ICBX. Integrated computer-based branch exchange. See *PABX.*

IEEE. Institute of Electrical and Electronics Engineers. A professional organization that has defined several I/O standards.

IEEE-488. A hardware interface made popular by Hewlett-Packard. Used mainly for test equipment and not commonly used for communications.

IEEE-802. Local-network standards committee of the IEEE.

interface. The interconnection point—usually between equipment.

I/O. Input-output.

I/O-bound. Describing a condition where the operation of the I/O port is the limiting factor in program execution.

International Standards Organization (ISO). Best known for the development of a network model called the Open System Interconnection (OSI) Reference Model.

Internet Protocol (IP). A standard protocol for communicating between devices on different networks. NBS and DOD have both published an IP standard. The two are very similar.

k. Abbreviation for *kilo,* meaning 1000; for example, a 1.2-kbps circuit operates at 1200 bits per second.

KSR. Keyboard send-receive. A terminal (particularly a printing terminal) with a keyboard.

LAN. Local area network.

LAP-B. Link Access Protocol, Balanced. A bit-oriented link-layer protocol defined as part of X.25 by CCITT. Very similar to HDLC and ADCCP.

leased line. A communications circuit reserved for the permanent use of a customer. Also called *private line.*

lightwave communications. Usually, communications using fiber-optic cables and light generated by lasers or light-emitting diodes (LEDs). Also may refer to systems using modulated light beams passing through the air between buildings or other adjacent locations.

link layer. The second layer in the ISO architecture. This layer performs the function of taking data from the higher layers, creating packets, and sending them accurately out the physical layer (layer 1).

local loop. The connection between the customer's premises and the telephone company's central office.

Loosely Coupled Network. A local-area network scheme from Control Data Corporation (CDC). The Loosely Coupled Network manages the data-link control, networking, and transport layers in the communications system. It is designed to allow computers from other major manufacturers to communicate with CDC systems.

low-speed modem. A modem operating at speeds up to 600 bps. See *medium-speed, high-speed,* and *wideband modem.*

mainframe. A large centralized computer.

mark. A signaling condition equal to a binary 1.

media. Plural of *medium.*

medium. The conduit used to move information: coaxial cable, fiber-optic cable, and so on.

medium-speed modem. A modem operating between 600 and 2400 bps. See *low-speed, high-speed,* and *wideband modem.*

message switching. A switching technique using a message store-and-forward system. No dedicated path is established. Rather, each message contains a destination address and is passed from source to destination through intermediate nodes. At each node, the entire message is received, stored briefly, and then passed on to the next node.

midsplit. A type of broadband cable system in which the available frequencies are split into two groups, one for transmission and one for reception. Requires a frequency converter.

modem. Modulator-demodulator. A device that translates between electrical signals and some other means of signaling. Typically, a modem translates between direct-current signals from a computer or terminal and analog signals sent over telephone lines. Other modems handle radio frequencies and lightwaves.

modem eliminator. A wiring device to replace two modems. It connects equipment over a distance of up to several hundred feet. Also called a *null modem.*

modulation. A process of varying signals to represent intelligent information. The frequency, amplitude, or phase of a signal may be modulated to represent an analog or digital signal.

multipoint line. A single communications link for two or more devices shared by one computer and more than one terminal. Use of this line requires a polling mechanism. Also called a multidrop line.

NAK. A control code indicating that a character or block of data was not properly received. See *ACK.*

NAU. See *Network-addressable unit.*

network. A communications system made up of various stations. Use of the term *network* assumes interaction among the stations.

Network-addressable unit (NAU). In SNA, a unit that can be the source and end of messages.

network layer. The third layer in the ISO architecture. Responsible for maintaining control over the communications links and routing data across one or more communications links. It accepts messages from the source, converts them into packets, and directs the packets to the destination.

node. A terminal location in a communications system. A node may also be a switching point where information changes format or mode of transmission.

OA. Office automation.

Open System Interconnection (OSI). A model developed by the International Standards Organization (ISO) to describe a network open to equipment from various manufacturers.

PABX. Private automated branch exchange. A telephone communications system serving a specific location such as an office or building. The word *automated* indicates that users may place and receive their own calls with little or no operator intervention. Modern PABX systems may include the ability to switch and pass digital signals.

packet. A string of characters that includes the source address, the destination address, and the message itself. Different systems utilize different-size packets.

packet switching. A method of transmitting messages through a communications network in which long messages are subdivided into short packets with a maximum length. The packets are then transmitted as in message switching. Usually, packet switching is more efficient and rapid than message switching.

parity. In ASCII, a check of the total number of 1 bits in a character. A final eighth bit is set so the count, when transmitted, is always even or always odd. This even or odd state can easily be checked at the receiving end.

passive head end. A device that connects the two broadband cables of a dual-cable system. It does not provide frequency translation.

PBX. Private branch exchange. A telephone system serving a specific location that relies on operator intervention to place or receive calls.

parallel transmission. Simultaneous transmission of bits down parallel wires. For example, byte parallel transmission requires eight wires. See *serial transmission*.

PCM. See *pulse code modulation*.

PDN. See *public data network*.

phase modulation. A method of modulation by varying the phase relationship of an analog signal.

physical layer. The lowest layer in the ISO architecture. Concerns itself with the voltage levels, speed, and signaling used between equipment.

polling. A method of controlling the transmission sequence of communicating devices by using an inquiry to the device asking if it wishes to transmit.

presentation layer. Layer 6 of the ISO architecture. Determines how the data are displayed. Concerned with format and visual presentation.

propagation delay. The delay between the time a signal enters a channel and the time it is received. This is normally insignificant in local networks, but it becomes a major factor in satellite communications.

protocol. A set of rules governing the transmission of information over a data channel.

PSDN. Packet-switched data network.

public data network. Usually refers to a government-controlled or national monopoly packet-switched network. This service is publically available to data processing users. See *VAN*.

pulse-code modulation (PCM). A common method for digitizing voice. The bandwidth required for a single digitized voice channel is 64 kbps.

reverse channel. An answer-back channel provided during half-duplex operation. Allows the receiving modem to send low-speed acknowledgments to the transmitting modem without breaking the half-duplex mode. Also used to arrange the turnaround between modems so that one ceases transmitting and the other begins.

RAM. Random-access memory. Also known as *read-write memory*. Usually able to accept user programs.

ring. A network topology in which the stations of the network are arranged (electrically) in a ring or circle.

RJE. Remote job entry. A processing technique allowing remote entry of what are essentially batch-processed jobs.

RO. Receive-only. A one-way device such as a printer, plotter, or graphics display.

ROM. Read-only memory.

RS-232-C. An electrical standard for the interconnection of equipment established by the Electrical Industries Association. The same as CCITT code V.24. RS-232-C is used for serial ports.

RS-449. A newer standard than RS-232-C, also used for serial communications. Eventually meant to replace RS-232-C, but backward compatibility is specified in RS-449.

SDLC. Synchronous Data-Link Control. A bit-oriented, link-layer communications protocol developed by IBM. Related to HDLC.

serial port. An I/O port that transmits data out one bit at a time. Contrasted to a parallel port, which transmits multiple (usually eight) bits simultaneously. RS-232-C is a common serial signaling protocol.

session. An interconnection between two stations for the purpose of moving information.

session layer. Layer 5 of the ISO architecture. Determines how the data received are to be routed and processed. Serves as an interface between applications programs and the communications systems.

slotted ring. An access method used in ring systems which involves passing an empty message frame around the system until a station fills it.

SNA. Systems Network Architecture. A communications model developed by IBM that integrates computer systems with data communications devices. This model describes functional layers in a manner similar to the OSI model.

space. The signal condition that equals a binary 0.

star. A network arrangement characterized by a central processor that communicates with outlying units arranged like the spokes of a wheel or a star. In the local-network context, the central processor is a specialized switch (PABX) that performs circuit switching.

start bit. A data bit used in asynchronous transmission to signal the beginning of a character and a busy channel. A space signal lasting only for the duration of one bit.

stop bit. A data bit used in asynchronous transmission to signal the end of a character and an idle channel. A mark signal lasting at least the duration of one bit.

store and forward. See *message switching*.

synchronous. A transmission system in which characters are synchronized by the transmission of initial synch characters. No stop or start bits are used.

strobe. An electrical signal calling for the transfer of information.

sync character. A character (two or more in bisync) sent from a transmitting station for the purpose of synchronizing the clocks in the transmitting and receiving stations.

TCAM. Telecommunications Access Method. An IBM system for controlling communications.

TCP. See *Transport Control Protocol.*

TDM. See *time-division multiplexing.*

telex. An international message service. Marketed in the United States by Western Union.

time-division multiplexing (TDM). A method of placing a number of signals on one communications circuit by allocating the available time among competing stations. Allocations may be on a microsecond basis.

token passing. An allocation scheme used in ring networks in which a very short all-clear message (token) is passed around the network until a station catches it and changes it to "Here comes a message." The token-passing scheme can also be used in bus networks. In this case, each station must know who is next after it and pass the token.

topology. An information industry buzzword meaning the physical design or shape of a system. Common topologies are the ring, star, and tree.

TP. See *Transport Protocol.*

transceiver. A communicating device capable of transmitting and receiving.

transmission control. The layer in SNA that controls sessions and manages communications.

Transport Control Protocol (TCP). A layer-4 protocol (see *transport layer*) developed by DOD and required on new DOD networks. Differs significantly from the NBS transport protocol.

transport layer. Layer 4 in the ISO architecture. Checks the received data, acknowledges receipt, and sends the data to a specific device (printer, terminal, or disk file).

Transport Protocol (TP). A layer-4 protocol (see *transport layer*) developed by the National Bureau of Standards. This protocol will probably be required on all new non-DOD government networks.

tree. Not a leafy thing that grows in the forest, but rather a network arrangement in which the stations hang off a common "branch," or data bus, like leaves.

TSO. Time-sharing option. An IBM system allowing various customers to use a computer system more or less simultaneously.

TTY. An abbreviation for electromagnetic printer (Teletype) equipment.

two-wire circuit. Usually a half-duplex circuit.

twisted pair. An electrical cable used for communications. Often used in PABX systems.

TWX. A message service provided by Western Union. It uses different terminal equipment from Telex, but the two systems are interconnected.

Universal Data-Link Control (UDLC). A packet protocol developed by Univac.

VAN. Value-added network. A privately owned packet-switched network whose services are sold to the public. See *PDN.*

Virtual Telecommunications Access Method (VTAM). One of the IBM access methods used on an SNA network.

voice channel. A transmission path usually limited to passing the bandwidth of the human voice (approx. 3 KHz).

WangNet. A local-network system from Wang Labs. WangNet is a broadband local network. Different bands of radio frequencies on the network are designed for different kinds of work. The HDLC packet format is used with the CSMA/CD access technique.

wideband. A channel or transmission medium capable of passing more frequencies than a standard 3-KHz voice channel.

wideband modem. A modem that operates over 9600 bps. See *high-speed modem.*

Wpm. Words per minute.

X.21. The physical interface description of X.25.

X.25. A packet-switching standard adopted by the CCITT. It defines the physical interface level, the frame level, and the network protocol level of the system.

Appendix A
Example of a CBX

Rolm offers a family of CBX products. The Rolm CBX started life as a telephone system and still emphasizes that role. But the use of the system for data communications is growing.

Figure A-1 The Rolm CBX has the capability to integrate voice and digital communications into the information-movement system. (Diagram courtesy of Rolm Corporation.)

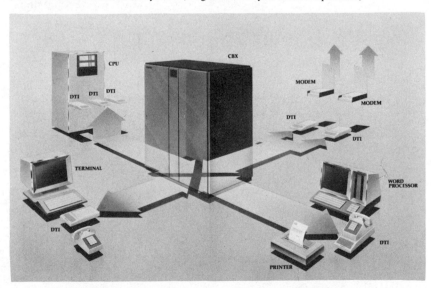

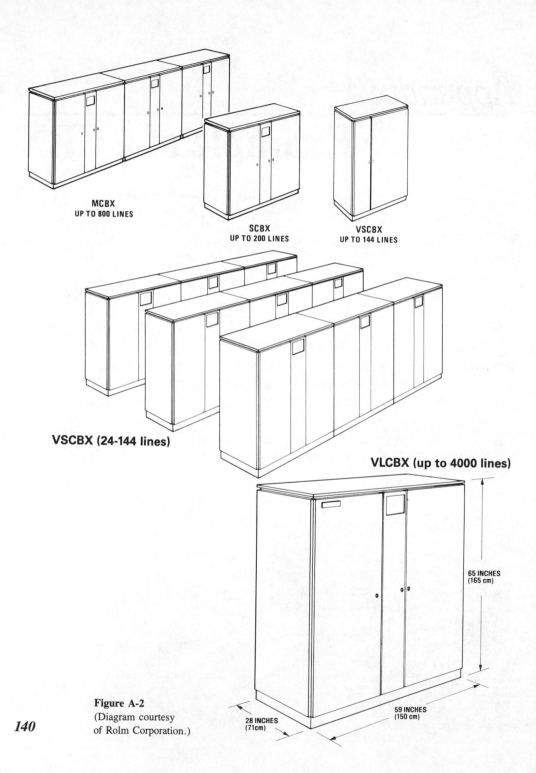

MCBX
UP TO 800 LINES

SCBX
UP TO 200 LINES

VSCBX
UP TO 144 LINES

VSCBX (24-144 lines)

VLCBX (up to 4000 lines)

65 INCHES
(165 cm)

28 INCHES
(71cm)

59 INCHES
(150 cm)

Figure A-2
(Diagram courtesy
of Rolm Corporation.)

140

SYSTEM DESCRIPTION

The system is of modular design, using one or more equipment cabinets as the central switching mechanism. Each cabinet consists of a set of racks, and each rack consists of a row of printed circuit boards. There are CPU, memory, and interface boards, these last used for establishing switched circuits. Redundancy of components, including the CPU, is possible even within a single cabinet. In the larger systems, the cabinets are hooked together by high-speed digital bus and configured so that loss of one portion of the system is isolated.

This design, based on the principles of modularity and redundancy, is highly reliable, overcoming one of the principal objections to the star topology of a CBX.

The interface boards are organized into groups, each group containing the logic needed to handle a number of lines of a certain type. These types include analog voice, digital voice, data, and trunks. Analog voice lines handle ordinary rotary or push-button phones. Since all the switching logic in the CBX is digital, the interface group for analog voice lines must contain a coder (for converting analog voice to digital) and a decoder (for the reverse operation). Digital voice lines are used with phones containing the coder-decoder logic (called a *codec*). Data lines of various speeds are used for computer and terminal equipment. Finally, trunk lines connect the CBX to the outside world.

SWITCHING LOGIC

Rolm uses a technique known as *time-division multiplexing (TDM)* for communications. Essentially, TDM involves the interleaving of bits from a number of sources so that they can share a common data path. In this case, the path is a high-speed bus that connects all the interface groups in a cabinet. For systems with multiple cabinets, there are also buses to connect the cabinets.

Time on the bus is organized into *time slots*. To establish a connection between two lines, the Rolm computer assigns unique, repetitive time slots on the common bus. The slots recur frequently enough to provide adequate data rate. Data is inserted on and removed from these time slots by the two connected interface boards.

A single phone call involves a series of connections and a number of "states." Consider, for example, a call from extension 226 to extension 280. The call is initiated when the phone with extension 226 goes off the hook. The CPU receives this information and establishes a connection with a tone generator; the call is placed in the dialing state by the CPU. When the first digit is dialed, the dial-tone connection is released. After the remaining digits are dialed, the CPU checks to see that 280 is a legitimate extension and is not busy. Extension 280 is rung and extension 226 is connected to a ring-back tone generator; the call is placed in the ringing state. When extension 280 goes off the hook, ringing and ring-back tone are released and the two extensions are connected; the call is placed in the connect state. When one of the parties hangs up, the connection is released and the call is terminated by the CPU.

DATA COMMUNICATIONS

The system architecture and switching logic of the Rolm CBX is well suited to data communications. The same wiring and system are used for data as for voice. The additional components needed are an inexpensive interface for the digital equipment, new interface boards in the CBX, and some additional software.

The unit for connecting digital data devices to the network is a *data-terminal interface (DTI)*. Since both the CBX and the device are digital, no modem is needed. The DTI can transmit asynchronous data at selectable speeds of from 110 bps to 19.2 kbps, at distances up to 1 mile from the CBX. Synchronous data transmission is not supported; hence, synchronous terminals and other synchronous devices cannot be connected to the CBX.

Connections are established from a DTI in much the same way as from a telephone. The user pushes a toggle switch to originate the call. The message "ENTER NUMBER" is displayed on the connected terminal. The user enters the number on the terminal keyboard; this number is sent into the CBX by the DTI. A DTI can also be placed in automatic-answer mode. This would typically be done for computer attachments.

The new software and interface boards handle the logic peculiar to data transmission. The most notable difference between data and digital voice transmission on the Rolm CBX is that data may be transmitted at a variety of speeds. Hence, the number of time slots assigned to a data connection is variable.

When access to and from remote terminals and computers is needed, modems are required for transmitting over external analog phone lines. To avoid the cost of equipping each device with a modem, Rolm offers a modem pool. All devices attached to DTIs can be automatically connected to a modem to access resources remote from the CBX. Similarly, remote terminals with modems can connect to the computers on site through the CBX by dialing a number assigned to the modem pool. This capability can be used to reduce the number of modems on site by a factor of two or more, depending on the relative frequency of external connections.

EXAMPLE

Let us consider a recent installation of a Rolm system for an aircraft company. The customer had a mainframe computer with a front-end processor to handle terminal traffic. Forty synchronous terminals were connected, using dial-up lines. Typically, these terminals were in offices that had only one phone, so that the user had to tie up his only line to use the time-sharing system. Finally, the customer had two stand-alone word processors.

The customer had the following needs: First, anticipated growth required more terminals, and the customer wanted an alternative to the high-cost synchronous terminals. Second, the word processing load was increasing rapidly. The customer wanted to centralize the word processing function (an organizational change) and provide a number of word processing work stations distributed for use by secretaries. Finally, the customer wanted a new telephone system to accommodate expansion.

The Rolm CBX provided the solution. First, for the terminals, sixteen ports on the front-end processor were hooked into the CBX. The customer bought 40 low-cost asynchronous terminals; since these also attached to the CBX, they required no modem. The terminals were placed in offices throughout the building. The original synchronous terminals remained attached directly to the front-end processor. Second, Rolm recommended the purchase of a centralized word processor with six ports and eighteen work stations. It was assumed that the peak loading on the system would be six work stations. If demand increased, additional ports could easily be added to the word processor. Finally, the existing telephone system was replaced with the CBX.

Little additional wiring was needed beyond that already installed in the building.

The customer purchased a CBX consisting of three cabinets with the following equipment:

448	Single-line telephones (wired for 580)
37	ETS100 telephones (wired for 60)
1	Attendant's console
36	Two-way central office trunks (wired for 64)
24	Direct inward dialing trunks
40	Data terminal interfaces (wired for 64)

Appendix B

Example of
a Broadband System

In 1981, AMDAX Corporation announced a broadband local-network product called CableNet. CableNet was designed to meet a number of objectives. First, AMDAX wanted to provide a general-purpose data communications service, with all of the properties we've discussed before: reliability, high capacity, cost-effectiveness, and so on. Second, CableNet was designed for interbuilding as well as intrabuilding communications. Third, the network was designed to support all types of communications simultaneously—data, video, audio—without exhausting capacity. Finally, the network supported a variety of protocols.

FEATURES

Using a tree topology, the CATV cable of CableNet can be routed throughout an organization's structure (or structures) in any configuration. CableNet can span an area of 2,000 square miles, with user terminal devices located as far as 50 miles apart.

AMDAX offers three services on the cable: switched, dedicated, and general.

The switched service allows multiple user devices to share access of a single transmission medium. The service allocates time on the bus

145

LOCAL AREA
COMMUNICATIONS NETWORK

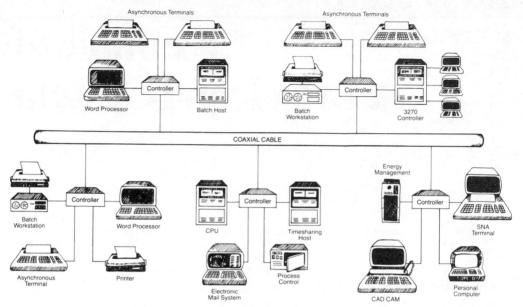

Figure B-1 The AMDAX broadband cable system has the capability to interface with a number of different kinds of communicating devices. (Diagram courtesy of AMDAX Corporation.)

dynamically to meet the needs of the attached devices. Two channels using this service are provided. Each can support 16,000 attached devices, for a total capacity of 32,000 devices.

Operating on the same broadband cable, the dedicated service supports dedicated multidrop or point-to-point data links that require full bandwidth (up to 56 kbps) on a sustained basis. This service is analogous to a user's securing a dedicated leased line from the phone company and is cost-effective for heavy traffic loads. The service reserves a small portion of the cable's frequency capacity for exclusive use by a dedicated link. Up to 252 links can be provided.

The general service can be used for general applications such as teleconferencing, paging, music, and closed-circuit TV. Twenty channels on the cable are allocated for these applications. No special AMDAX hardware is used.

For data communications, using both switched and dedicated

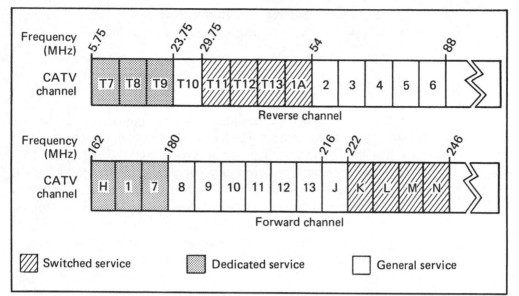

CableNet frequency spectrum. *Switched service uses 48 MHz, and dedicated service uses 36 MHz of CableNet's 166–MHz total bandwidth, leaving half the bandwidth available for general service.*

Figure B-2 The CableNet frequency-allocation plan. Switched services use 48 MHz and dedicated services use 36 MHz of CableNet's 166 MHz total bandwidth. The remaining frequencies are available for other user services.

$(23.75 - 5.75) +$
$(180 - 162) = 36$

services, devices connect to the network via data exchange (DAX) interface units. The device interfaces are standard RS-232-C, with selectable speeds up to 19.2 kbps for switched and 56 kbps for dedicated.

Protocols supported by the DAX include asynchronous, bisync, SLDC, HDLC, and X.25. These protocols are handled transparently; that is, to the device, it appears that it is attached to a modem on a dial-up (switched) or leased (dedicated) line. Hence, no hardware or software modification is required to hook the device into the network.

For any two devices on the network to communicate, they must establish a "connection." For the dedicated service, connections are preconfigured. For the switched service, two types of connections are offered: permanent virtual circuits (PVC) and switched virtual calls (SVC).

PVC defines a permanent connection between two devices and is set by a network manager. This would be used, for example, between a word processing terminal and the word processing system. SVC allows any device to communicate with any other device on the network. The user can select a different destination for each session. A simple command language is provided for establishing connections.

NETWORK OPERATION

CableNet use a midsplit broadband cable configuration. Devices are connected to the system via DAXs. These are microprocessor-based units that communicate by sending packets to the head end of the cable on the reverse channel and receiving packets on the forward channel.

The CableNet executive is located at the head end. It receives packets transmitted on the reverse channel, translates them to a higher frequency, and transmits them on the forward channel.

The executive is also responsible for resource allocation, using a reservation protocol. Unlike CSMA/CD, this protocol requires centralized control. However, it also provides better performance.

The reservation protocol works roughly like this. Time is divided into "slots" of fixed duration. When a DAX has data to transmit, it sends a request to the executive for a number of slots. The executive reserves some future slots for that DAX and sends an acknowledgment, telling the DAX which slots it can use.

Acting as a communications controller and modem, the DAX transforms the data rate and protocol of the subscriber device to that of the cable and vice versa. Data on the channel are available to all DAXs, which screen packets for reception based on address. The DAX performs the following functions:

> Accepts data from attached devices.
> Buffers the data until cable access is granted (by reservation).
> Transmits the data in addressed packets.
> Scans each packet on the cable for ones addressed to itself.
> Reads packets into a buffer.
> Transmits data to attached devices at the proper data rate.

EXAMPLE

A large financial institution was faced with the following requirements when it moved two departments to a new forty-story building.

First, there was a video requirement. Access to the first fifteen floors was to be restricted for security reasons. The facilities department required cabling to support video cameras on each floor, monitored by a centralized surveillance center on the first floor. Provision for expanding security restrictions to an additional five to eight floors was also required.

Second, there was a data requirement. Each department would have its own computer center, one on the sixteenth floor and one on the thirty-first floor. Terminals were to be installed throughout twenty-eight floors of the building with access to the computer-center mainframes.

The initial data processing requirement was to install 120 terminals, with additional terminals installed at a rate of ten per month. While the general location of terminal equipment was predetermined, individual managers and supervisors would determine the exact locations. It was anticipated that one or two terminals per month would be relocated.

Two alternatives were considered:

1. Install coaxial cable for the security system and twisted-pair wire with data switches for the data system.
2. Install a broadband local network for both requirements.

For alternative 1, the following would be needed:

Cable, material, installation for 15 stories
Twisted 6-pair wire for data circuits for 28 stories
1 data switch
2 data concentrators (1000 less capacity) (1 per 14 floors)
2 9600-baud lines and modems (between concentrators and switch)
120 data ports
240 limited-distance modems

For alternative 2, AMDAX quoted the following:

Cable, material, installation for 40 stories
CableNet executive
40 switched DAXs (160 ports)

Although the DAX is considerably more expensive than a data port and modem, the overall cost of the AMDAX alternative was 30 percent less than the twisted-pair approach. The savings on cabling and the lack of a data switch and data concentrators made up the difference. Furthermore, the customer is now in a position easily to expand both the surveillance system and the data system with no additional cabling.

Appendix C

Ethernet

The most widely known local network is Ethernet. An experimental version of Ethernet was developed in the mid-1970s by Xerox Corporation. The network used the CSMA/CD protocol on a 3-Mbps baseband cable. Xerox's announced purpose for this system was to develop a de facto industry standard for local networks. Xerox strengthened its hand by enlisting Digital Equipment Corporation and Intel to participate in the development of specifications and components. In 1980, the Ethernet specification was published; its principal difference from the experimental system was the use of a 10-Mbps transfer rate.

Ethernet consists of four types of components: cable, transceiver, controller, and repeater.

The cable used is a special coaxial cable suited for baseband transmission. This differs from broadband systems, which use standard CATV cable.

Attachment to the cable is by means of a transceiver. The *transceiver* is a simple device that connects directly to the cable and provides both the electronics which transmit and receive digital signals on the cable and the required electrical isolation.

Connected to the transceiver is the controller. The *controller* contains the logic for the CSMA/CD protocol and for interfacing to attached devices.

150

Repeaters are used to overcome certain limitations of the Ethernet cable. The cable is limited to a maximum length of 500 meters with a maximum of 100 connections. Further, only straight segments of cable can be used; no branching is allowed. To extend the length, number of stations, and topology, repeaters may be used to connect cable segments. The repeater is connected to two segments and retransmits all received signals from each segment to the other. A maximum of two

Figure C-1 This diagram shows how an Ethernet network may be integrated throughout an office building. (Diagram courtesy of Xerox Corporation. All rights reserved.)

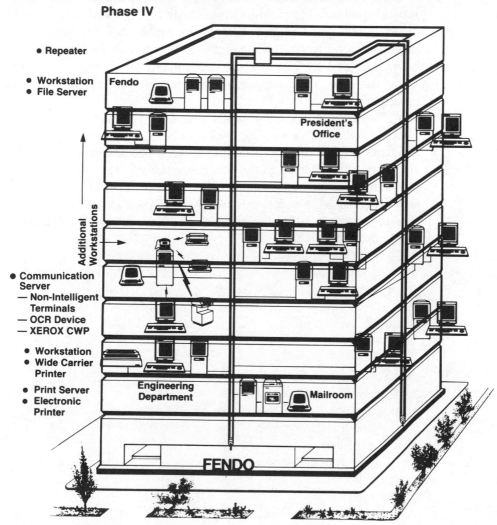

repeaters may be in the signal path between any two stations on the network.

The specification for Ethernet has been published in the hopes of encouraging mass production of controller chips, thus driving down the price of connection and promulgating Ethernet as a de facto standard. Xerox touts Ethernet as the "plug-in" solution that can be used to connect all types of data processing equipment from different vendors. Potential customers have been led to believe that true interconnectability was on the way.

Unfortunately, this manager's dream is not a reality. The local network protocol specification covers only layers 1 and 2 of the OSI model. The higher-level protocols, layers 3 through 7, are required for interconnectability. And, while higher-level protocols for Ethernet have been developed by Xerox, these are unlikely to be widely adopted since national standards are being developed by the federal government.

Furthermore, even for layers 1 and 2, Ethernet is not alone. National standards for local networks are being developed not only for baseband but for broadband and ring as well. The baseband standard is similar but not identical to the Ethernet standard. The broadband and ring standards are significantly different. Low-cost chips for these national standard protocols will soon be available. Hence, the de facto Ethernet standard will be in competition with the official local-network standards.